SCHÖNING'S TRAVEL GUIDE

S0-ABK-832

NUREMBERG

Text: Wolfgang Kootz, revised and expanded by Karin Ecker
Concept: Boris Fengler
Photos: Archiv Edm. von König Verlag, S. Löhe, A. Cowin,
Nuremberg Toy Museum, Nuremberg City Museum
Our thanks go to the company Haeberlein-Metzger
Maps: Huber Kartographie, Munich,
VGN (Greater Nuremberg Transport Association)
Editorial staff: S. Gödecke

Overall production and © Copyright by
SCHÖNING GmbH & CO KG
An der Hülshorst 5 · 23568 LÜBECK
☎ (04 51) 31 03-0 · Fax: (04 51) 3 52 83
E-mail: info@schoening-verlag.de
Internet: www.schoening-verlag.de
ISBN: 978-3-89917-281-2
8th edition

PEFC

Contents

Welcome to Nuremberg!

The city lies in the sandy plain of the central Franconian basin and is sometimes referred to as the "secret capital" of Bavaria and is in fact with its almost 500,000 inhabitants the second largest city in that state. The river Pegnitz divides the old town into its Sebald and Lorenz districts, named after the town's two main churches. Above both rises the medieval castle, the city's "crown." Perhaps or

The protective wall in front of the round Sinwell Tower once shielded the Imperial Castle against the Burgrave's Castle

just because the soil around is unfavorable to agricultural pursuits, Nuremberg has developed rather from the hard work and business sense its citizens have possessed, characteristics which were present even in the Middle Ages and which have contributed to making the city one of Germany's most important centers. In the "jewel case of the German Empire," famous artists as Albrecht Dürer and Hans Sachs, Veit Stoß and Peter Vischer, Martin Behaim and Peter Henlein flourished. The name Nuremberg itself calls to mind Lebkuchen (gingerbread) and fried sausages, toys, The Meistersingers, the Nuremberg Funnel, its Christmas Market, Gothic art treasures, its mighty city walls and far distant Imperial Diets, but also perhaps its most recent history with the Nazi Party Rallies, the Nuremberg Laws and the trial of top Nazi criminals. The attraction of the city lies in its contrasts between that which has been preserved and the living spirit of the town.

A Short History of Nuremberg

16th July 1050	"Norenberc" mentioned for the first time in an official document, on the occasion of the release of the serf Sigena by Emperor Heinrich III.
After middle of 11th cen.	First buildings of the Burgraves' Castle, among others a public hall on the site of the eastern part of today's "Palas."
1140–1180	Extension of the Staufen emperor's castle under Friedrich Barbarossa.
1181	Emperor Friedrich I refers to Nuremberg as "Our City" (Castrum nostrum) in a document.
1191/92	Count Friedrich III von Hohenzollern becomes Burgrave Friedrich I of Nuremberg by marriage.
1219	Emperor Friedrich III issues the "Letter of Freedom." This first city privilege subjects Nuremberg to the rule of the empire.
1273	The lands belonging to the Hohenzollerns become heritable.
1332	Emperor Ludwig the Bavarian confirms the exemption from duties and taxes for the people of Nuremberg in 70 places within the empire. He sojourns in the city 74 times.
1348/49	Tradesmen's Revolt. Recapture by the noble families of the town is successful.
1349	Emperor Karl IV permits the destruction of the Jewish Quarter to make room for a market place. 562 of the approx. 1500 inhabitants are killed.
1356	Karl IV signs the imperial law "Golden Bull." The seven electors elect the new king who is obliged to hold the first Imperial Diet in Nuremberg. Karl IV sojourns 52 times in his favorite city.
1377	The town erects the "Luginsland" Tower.
ca. 1400	The last city wall around today's Old Town is completed, the moat is built by 1452.

1415	Burgrave Friedrich VI is bequeathed the Brandenburg March.
1420	Christoph Laiminger, curator of the Dukes of Bavaria, has the Burgraves' Castle burned to the ground.
1424	Emperor Sigismund, one of the younger sons of Karl IV, decrees that the imperial insignia be kept in Nuremberg forever. They remain in the city until 1796.
1427	Burgrave Friedrich VI sells his devastated property and other rights to the city for 120,000 guilders.
1442	Emperor Friedrich III visits Nuremberg six times in all.
1449–53	The first Markgraves' War. Albrecht Achilles von Brandenburg-Ansbach, son of Friedrich IV, demands the property formerly belonging to his family back, and attacks the fortifications with over 7000 men, but fails to conquer it.
after 1470	The city experiences its cultural peak with Veit Stoß, Adam Kraft, Martin Behaim, Peter Vischer, Willibald Pirckheimer, Albrecht Dürer and Hans Sachs.
1487	Emperor Friedrich III holds a brilliant imperial diet.
1525	The Reformation in Nuremberg.
1533	The plague strikes again: "Hans Tuchmacher and 14 children die in a single day." Further outbreaks in 1562 (5754 deaths), 1585 (9186 deaths), 1633/34 (15661 deaths).
1543	Last Imperial Diet takes place in Nuremberg.
1552	Second Margraves' War: Albrecht "Alcibiades," Margrave of Kulmbach, fails to conquer the fortification but destroys 2 cities, 170 villages, 3 monasteries, 19 castles, 75 residential palaces or mansions, 28 mills, 33 smiths' workshops and 3000 acres of forest in the Nuremberg area. After the war, Nuremberg has a debt of 3.5 million guilders.

1618–48	The Thirty Years War: Nuremberg remains neutral and protects itself behind its thick walls from the effects of the war. More than 35,000 people perish, but many of them between 1632 and 1634 from typhus, dysentery and the plague. Nuremberg's decline continues as the result of further debt.
1623	The university of the imperial city of Nuremberg was founded in Altdorf (it existed until 1809). An Academy founded in Nuremberg in 1526 was transferred to Altdorf in 1575.
1649	The Treaty of Nuremberg marks the end of the Thirty Years War.
ca. 1800	Nuremberg is discovered by Romanticism.
1806	The city is annexed to the newly founded Kingdom of Bavaria.
1835	The first German railway runs from Nuremberg to Fürth.
19th century	Nuremberg develops into an industrial town.
1836–46	Construction of the Ludwig-Donau-Main-Kanal with a length of 177 km.
1927	First Rally of the National Socialist Party in Nuremberg.
1935	The "Nuremberg Laws" are passed. These rob the Jews of their place in society and state.
1938	The last Nazi Party Rally is attended by about one million people. Exhibition of the imperial insignia.
Jan. 2, 1945	Over 90% of the Old Town is destroyed in an air raid. 1829 people lose their lives.
1945–49	The "Nuremberg Trials" of the major representatives of the Nazi regime are held.
1950	The first International Toy Fair takes place.
1955	Opening of Nuremberg Airport at the Kraftshofer Forst, following the destruction of the airport at the Marienberg during the war.
1961	Foundation of the University of Erlangen-Nuremberg. Today, it is Bavaria's second largest university with over 21,000 students.

1966	The reconstruction of the old part of Nuremberg is for the most part completed.
1972	Inauguration of the Staatshafen (harbor) on the Europe Canal which was completed in 1992 and links the River Main with the Danube. It was planned primarily for commercial shipping, but the waterway's significance as a tourist attraction is constantly increasing.
1972	The first underground railway section with a length of 3.7 km is opened for public transportation. Meanwhile, Line U1 from Langwasser to Fürth and Line U2 from Röthenbach to the airport are completed. Extension of the underground railway system started with the construction of Line U3.
1973	Inauguration of the new Messezentrum (Trade Fair Center) Nuremberg in Münchener Straße.
1993	Inauguration of the extension building of the German National Museum in Münchener Straße as well as the work of art "Way of Human Rights" created by Dani Karavan in Kartäusergasse where the main entrance of the museum is now located.
1995	The 1st International Nuremberg Human Rights Award is given to Sergej Kowaljow. This award is granted by the city of Nuremberg every two years to persons committed to the realization of human rights.
1999	The Music Academy becomes the "University of Music Nuremberg-Augsburg."
2000	The "New Museum Nuremberg" – State Museum of Art and Design is opened.
2000	The "Documentation Center of the National Socialist Party Rally Grounds" is opened in the northern building of the Congress Hall.
2001	The city of Nuremberg is awarded the UNESCO prize for human rights education.
2003	The City Theaters Nuremberg become the "State Theater Nuremberg."

A TOUR ROUND OLD NUREMBERG

For a medieval city, Nuremberg is an enormously extensive town (1.77 km²) and all the many places of interest which are distributed throughout the old part of the city are too numerous to be covered in one day and so must, unfortunately, remain undiscovered. For this reason, our "little tour," which has the day-tourist in mind, is limited to the "musts" which, as we suggest, include visits to the interior of both main churches, that of St. Sebald and St. Lorenz. Strictly speaking, only those who are able to spend several days in this Franconian metropolis can gain a comprehensive impression of the cultural heritage either created here or brought here. Your tour can therefore be referred to as an "extended tour," and includes above all a visit to the castle interior, a number of museums, the area around the Egidienkirche (Egidien Curch) and the cemeteries which lie outside the city wall and can be reached by car.

1 The Castle

Our tour starts at the **Castle**, the city's landmark and place of origin. Passing through the **Vestner Gate** from the north or up the steep way with its "Heaven's Gate" from the city side, we proceed first to the highest point within the precincts, the inner courtyard. Here, we find ourselves in the center of the most heavily fortified part of the building, the **Kaiserburg** (Imperial Castle). This is where Emperor Heinrich III built the first fortress on the center section of these precipitous crags before 1050 in order to secure crown lands. Since the medieval Holy Roman Empire had no capital, the rulers and their entourage traveled from one palatinate to the next and held their Imperial Diets and trials. A castellan was appointed in Nuremberg to conduct the emperor's business and safeguard his interests. These officials are first mentioned in 1107, when the brothers Konrad and Gottfried von Raabs (Lower Austria) are named as witnesses in an imperial document with the surname "von Nürnberg." From 1191 on, following the

The Walpurgis Chapel of the Burgrave's Castle and the Sinwell Tower

extinction of the Raab family, Friedrich von Zollern became Burgrave by marriage with a residence in what is today called the **Burgraves' Castle**.

Just how important Nuremberg was at this time is indicated by the fact that every German emperor between 1050 and 1571 visited here, Emperor Karl IV as many as 52 times. Altogether there were more than 300 visits of German rulers in Nuremberg as well as numerous splendid Imperial Diets and assemblies at court. The imperial decree "Golden Bull" issued in 1356 provided for every newly elected German king to hold his first Imperial Diet at Nuremberg. Since 1313, the citizens of Nuremberg had the obligation to upkeep the castle but also the prerogative of maintaining their own castle garrison there during the absence of the emperor.

The inner courtyard ends with the elongated building of the **Palas** to the south, which was completely rebuilt in the 15th century and extended by an annex on the western side, thus gaining the appearance it has today. In addition to the two large halls in the main building, two residential rooms for the emperor were thus obtained. The last building to the west of the courtyard was the 'Kemenate' (Ladies' Quarters), to the north the courtyard ends at the defensive wall and to the east there is the castellan's building.

The Kemenate was destroyed in the bomb hail during World War II and later reconstructed. Today, it houses the Kaiserburg Museum (Imperial Castle Museum) as dependency of the German National Museum. It shows the architectural history and significance of the Imperial Palace as well as military and arms technology from the Middle Ages to the 19th century.

Passing now through an archway decorated with coats of arms, we come to the forecourt of the Imperial Castle

left:
The Twin Chapel from the east including the so-called Heathen Tower

right:
The well house and the secretary's building with forecourt of the Imperial Castle

bottom:
The "Deep Well" was hewn 50 m deep into the rock

which is surrounded by a row of half-timbered, sandstone buildings which begin immediately to the right with a **double chapel** whose upper floor served the emperor and court while the lower floor was reserved for his knights. From the tower onwards, the lower story dates all the way back to the 12th century. In the center of this court there is a well house (1563) with the **Tiefer Brunnen** (Deep Well) which was hewn 50 meters deep into the rock. To secure the water supply, this well is presumed to have been built when the first edifices of the Imperial Castle were erected. Even today, it maintains an average level of three meters. During a guided tour of the castle, the visitor can look down into the well. Two picturesque half-timbered houses from the 15th and 16th

centuries form the north-eastern corner of the courtyard; these are the secretary's building and accounting house at the foot of the mighty **Sinwell Tower** (sinwel = round). The round castle keep originates from the 12th century, the upper part, however, was only built around 1560. From the top one can enjoy a panoramic view over the rest of the castle and the city below.

The "Sinwell Tower" is the keep, i.e. the Imperial Castle's main tower

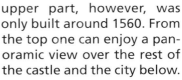

Those who are interested in doing more than a one-day tour of the town should not miss taking part in a guided tour of the **interior** of the Imperial Castle.

The Romanesque twin chapel dating from the late 12th century is the most important building within the castle. The stocky pillars of the lower chapel are in charming contrast to the slender marble ones of the emperor's place of worship whose arches give the impression of being weightless. The painting of the imperial gallery was accomplished by Hans Springinklee about 1520.

The elongated Knights' Hall situated on the ground floor of the castle's main building is roofed by a mighty wooden ceiling supported by thirty crossbeams whose trusses, running lengthways down the room, are in turn held in place by five oak supports. The window front facing the city has two bends and thus follows the shape of the castle rock. After ascending a wooden stairway we discover the **Emperor's Hall** on the second floor which has the same layout as the hall below. The late Gothic portal situated in the east face wall leads, like that of the Knights' Hall, to the twin chapel. Like the ceiling there, the ceiling in this upper chamber produces a much less weighty effect on the observer. The wooden beading still retains the imperial colors, yellow and black. Paintings of German emperors and princes adorn the walls. From here one has a magnificent view over Nuremberg's Old Town.

Imperial residence on the upper floor of the "Palas"

Imperial residence on the upper floor of the "Palas"

The adjoining rooms of the western annex came into being in 1487 under Friedrich III. The wooden wall paneling of the imperial reception hall as well as the impressive painted ceiling with its huge imperial eagle stem from this period, and both were saved from fire in 1945. Other appointments for the visitor to admire are pieces of Renaissance furniture, as loans from the German National Museum and several elaborate tiled stoves from the 16th and 17th centuries which were installed here in the 19th century.

Through the forecourt and the area referred to as "Freiung," we reach the oldest part of the fortress, the **Burggrafenburg** (Burgrave's Castle). In 1192, this passed by marriage into the possession of the House of Zollern who tried to extend their power from here into Franconian territory. As can be anticipated, this led to friction with the imperial city which, as we recall, maintained soldiery in the Imperial Castle. In the 14th century the city erected a protective wall in front of the keep together with all those parts connecting it to the north and south including the Vestner Gate, so that the military force within the castle had control of both entrances. The greatest affront against the burgrave, however, was the construction of a sturdy tower which the city built in just 40 days right in front of the castle in 1377. Since the burgrave's complaints to the emperor fell upon deaf ears, it came to war between the parties and the occupation of the Burgrave's Castle in 1388/89. To cap it all, the castle, which had been later returned to its owner, was burned to the ground in 1420 in the course of a feud between neighbors. Friedrich VI of the House of Hohenzollern, who in the meantime had appropriated the Mark Brandenburg, had in any case other interests and so the ruin and several rights were sold to the town in 1427 for 120,000 guilders. Nevertheless, two of his successors, Princes of Ansbach, and at least according to title Burgraves of Nuremberg, tried to wrench the ruins from its possession, but in spite of 20 allied dukes, 15 bishops including 7000 counts, lords, knights and squires, the city was conquered neither in the 1st (1449–53) nor in the 2nd Margraves' War (1552).

The ground upon which we stand at the moment between the walls of the Imperial Castle and the Counts' Castle used to be called 'Freiung' which approximates the word 'freedom.' When, in the Middle Ages, a criminal had succeeded in getting as far as this, he was granted the imperial city's right to asylum. The Burgraves' Castle, razed to the ground in 1420, was never rebuilt. Only the **Walpurgis Chapel** opposite the wall, the castle custodian's dwelling next to the north gate, the former keep and the pentagonal tower have remained intact. The latter probably dates back to the middle of the 12th century and is the oldest building of Nuremberg. Its peculiar layout is the result of adding a triangular reinforcement to the original, over 2.5 m thick walls on the side facing the enemy. The upper floors together with the modest wooden corner-piece were added after the fire of 1420. At the outermost eastern edge of the complex we can see the **"Lugins-**

land" ('Look Across Country'), erected in 1377 as a watchtower for the city. The gap between the two towers was filled in 1494–95 by the massive proportions of the **Imperial Stables**. Grain was stored in the six upper floors, and the building also served as stables for the emperor's horses. This work by the master mason, Hans Beheim the Elder, included results in a 200 m long enclosed castle complex which has bestowed an unmistakable silhouette upon the city. Today, the former stable building serves as a youth hostel.

Pentagonal tower, with the Imperial Stables and Luginsland behind it

Looking out from the 'Freiung' we gain an all-embracing view of the city's Old Town with the high, almost identical twin towers of its principal churches, St. Sebald and St. Lorenz. They gave their names to the two parts of the city which constitute the Old Town of Nuremberg, Sebalder Stadt, lying below the castle, and Lorenzer Stadt, situated south of the river. The confusion of roofs of the Old Town is demarcated at four places by impreguable round towers which, in days gone by, stood guard over the city's gates.

Castle
Tel. 09 11/22 57 26,
open October to March
10 a.m. – 4 p.m.,
April to September
9 a.m. – 6 p.m.

Kaiserburgmuseum
Tel. 09 11/2 00 95 40,
e-mail: info@gnm.de,
Internet: www.kaiserburg-museum.de,
open October to March 10 a.m. – 4 p.m.,
April to September 9 a.m. – 6 p.m.

Let us take the descent on the town side. As we go down we will be able to see the rock on which the castle stands. At the end of this steep path we turn right into 'Am Öl-berg' (Mount of Olives Lane), a street which closely follows the course of the south wall of the castle above. At the end of this street we enter the bastions which, in times of peace, served as castle gardens and still serve that purpose today. If now we keep to the left, we come to steps at the end of the bastion grounds and from here we can get to the sentry walk which runs from here right up to Tier-gärtnertor. It is the only section in the whole of Nurem-berg – especially here at the level of the Tiergärtnertor-platz – which offers delightful views.

Towards the end of 'Am Ölberg' there are stairs to the left going down. The house at the end to the right is called **Pilatushaus** (House of Pilate) and stands on the corner. It is easily distinguishable by the statue of St. George in shi-ning armor. Here, at one time, the armorer, Hans Grüne-wald, had his workshop, the fine half-timbered house having been erected in 1489. In this north-western section of the Old Town especially, quite a number of old houses made of stone and half-timbered work survived the rav-ages of World War II.

Almost opposite the Pilatushaus we notice the harmony achieved between the heavily-beamed "Schranke" (first mentioned in 1632) and the more delicately-structured Dürerhaus (about 1450) and how they fit beautifully to-gether. The medieval atmosphere of the square is enhanc-ed by the presence of the fortified buildings on the north-western side. The ensemble is dominated by the **Tier-gärtnertorturm** (Zoo Gate Tower) which dates back to an earlier fortification of the city in the 13th century. Only the two upper floors with characteristic polygonal oriels and the pointed tower were added in 1516.

A special contrast is created by the modern sculpture of a larger than life-size hare surrounded by others of more usual proportions. The location on this lively square and

St. George, the dragon killer, as patron saint of the armor makers on the so-called House of Pilate, also called the "House of the Armored Man"

"Hommage à Dürer" – bronze sculpture by Jürgen Goertz (1984)

the title of the **sculpture** called **"Hommage à Dürer"** establishes a link to Dürer's masterful watercolor painting.

In 1509, Albrecht Dürer (1471–1528) bought the house named after him from the heirs of the astronomer, Bernhard Walter. The master lived and worked here until his death.

Tiergärtnertorplatz with view towards the house where Albrecht Dürer lived

The Dürerhaus illuminated by night

"Albrecht Dürer portrays Emperor Maximilian," painted by Carl Jäger (1886)

Today, the **Dürerhaus** serves as a museum in which the visitor is given a good idea of the environment in which the great master lived. The kitchen, for example, is still the original (except for the movable objects) and the richly-furnished parlor has been reconstructed in 16th century style. On the upper floor, there is a workshop with all the utensils a painter and engraver needed in the era of Dürer. Even a reproduction of the original printing press used for his woodcuts is exhibited here. Although no original works of art can be seen in this house, the careful selection of Dürer's copperplate engravings and copies of paintings still demonstrates the enormous influence Dürer had on the work of other artists. The multi-vision show "Albertus Durer Noricus" is presented in the adjoining modern edifice. It gives an introduction into the work of the master.

Dürerhaus

Albrecht-Dürer-Str. 39, open Tuesday to Sunday 10 a.m. – 5 p.m., Thursday 10 a.m. – 8 p.m., Tel. 09 11/2 31 25 68, e-mail: museen@stadt.nuernberg.de, Internet: www.museen.nuernberg.de

Through the Lanes and Alleys of the Old Town

Dürerstraße leads downwards between the Museum and the "Schranke." Other half-timbered houses are No. 24 and No. 6 in this lane. Yet others (Nos. 22 and 11) are decorated with charming oriel altar niches (Chörlein). We will come across still more of these romantic miniature oriels made of wood or stone in **"Füll"** into which we turn left at the end of Dürerstraße. Added to what we have already seen, we now discover a row of beautifully-wrought roof bays in houses Nos. 5, 7, and 9. For a patrician house of that era, house No. 6 is especially richly decorated with its oriel altar niche and bay window on the side facing the street, its two-story balustrade with tracery overlooking the courtyard, as was common in the 16th and 17th centuries.

The Weißgerbergasse with its half-timbered houses from the 15th, 16th and 17th centuries

Diagonally across between houses No. 5 and No. 7, a flight of steps leads down to the **Weinmarkt** (Wine Market). On the left we notice the oriel altar niches of houses Nos. 1 and 2. On house No. 6 we find an additional wooden balustrade with oriel altar niche and bay to the front of the house. Crossing the Wine Market and bearing right we reach **Weißgerbergasse**. Following this lane we come across a row of very charming old artisans' houses both of stone and timbering and decorated with altar niches and bay windows, which make it one of the most enjoyable lanes of Nuremberg's Old Town. This includes the view that we have of the city's fortifications down at the end of the lane and from Maxplatz. At this point, its stream divided by a small island, the River Pegnitz leaves the Old Town under the arches of a bridge protected by sentry walks, little towers, the Schleyer Tower and a small bulwark on its outer wall. Further inside, the **Kettensteg** (Chain Walk) dating back to 1824 links both banks of the river for pedestrians.

We, however, will traverse **Maxplatz** in the direction of the city. In the park area to our right we see the Tritonbrunnen (Triton's Fountain), which was erected in 1687 in memory of Emperor Leopold I's victory over the Turks. The key figure is the stone representation of Triton, one of Neptune's followers. The neoclassical fountain (1821) marks the end of the park area. The medallions are dedicated to Albrecht Dürer and Willibald Pirckheimer.

View of the romantic Weißgerbergasse

4 At the Henkersteg (Hangman's Way)

Diagonally across we find the sturdy building of the **Weinstadel** (Wine Vaults) (1446–48) which was originally used to accommodate lepers for three days during Holy Week. When the number of sick people declined in the 16th century, the building was also used to store wine and as a poor house. Today, it serves as a student hostel and belongs to the University of Erlangen-Nürnberg.

The Henkersteg, view from the Karlsbrücke

The elongated Weinstadel building with its overhanging, timbered upper floor and its heavy gable roof is one of the most important and spacious medieval half-timbered edifices which have remained preserved until today.

Looking from the Maxbrücke (Max Bridge), the 48 m long building, together with the Water Tower and **Henkersteg** (Hangman's Way), present an imposing overall ensemble. The buildings just mentioned are part of the penultimate fortification of the city built in the 13th/14th century at a time when it was deemed necessary to secure the river's exit by a roofed sentry walk over the bridge's arches. Beyond the Henkerstürmchen (Hangman's Little Tower), at the tip of the island, the old sentry walk has been replaced by a covered wooden bridge. Downstream from the Maxbrücke, we have a view of the last city wall and on the **"Kettensteg"** (Chain Walk) covered with wooden beams. Built by the mechanic, Johann Georg Kuppler, in 1824 it was the first iron suspension bridge in Germany and considered to be a technical masterpiece. On the left bank of the River Pegnitz, an architecturally attractive residential complex was built on the area of the Kreuzgassen quarter which was destroyed in World War II.

The gable of the Wine Vault; the Water Tower and the building bridging the River Pegnitz are part of the penultimate town fortification

Having crossed the bridge, the street leads us directly to **Unschlittplatz** (Unschlitt Square). The fountain with its decorative bagpiper was cast in bronze in 1880 according to a wooden model dating from the 16th century on show in the German National Museum. This bagpiper is typical of the "Nuremberg Style" or the "Old German Style" which was especially popular in the 19th century.

The picturesque group of houses to our right owes its continued existence to the initiative of an association of Nuremberg citizens. The two, half-timbered houses seem to want to hold up the narrow stone house in their midst. In contrast, the imperial city's grain store on the other side of the square, the Unschlitthaus, appears gigantic. Its massive roof area is punctuated by 76 dormer windows whose purpose is to ventilate the building's four floors. The two-story sandstone building was the first of three corn houses which master mason Hans Beheim the Elder put up for the city of Nuremberg around the year 1500. This simple functional building still accommodates city authorities today, for instance the Election Department and the pawnshop. The public office formerly occupying the building was the "Unschlittamt" (Tallow Fat Department) – it was a collecting point for cow and sheep fat, and this was how the building got its name.

The Kettensteg and Schlayer Tower framed by a quatrefoil of the Max Bridge's parapet

Leaving the stepped, gabled roof of the **Unschlitthaus**, we continue our tour along Obere Wörthstraße. Here, the narrow, weather-boarded façades dominate, some as half-timbering with dormer windows or oriel altar niches. Passing over the Obere Karlsbrücke (1728) we come to the island called **"Trödelmarkt"** (Flea Market). The obelisks on the central pillar of the bridge carry an eagle and a dove representing war and peace. From here we can look down to the picturesque Holzsteg (Wood Path) and up to the Fleischbrücke (Meat Bridge). It was built between 1596 and 1598 following the design of the Rialto Bridge in Venice.

On the island we keep to the right and leave it via Schleifersteg (Schleifer Path). In front of the so-called "Fleischhaus" (Meat House), built as a slaughterhouse for the imperial city in 1571, we turn left into Winklerstraße which leads straight to St. Sebald´s Church.

5 The Toy Museum
(Extended Tour)

Crossing Augustinergasse and walking through Schuster-gasse (Shoemaker's Lane) we catch sight of the richly ador-ned Renaissance façade of the city's **Toy Museum** (about 1610). Only this façade with the Baroque oriel altar niche from 1720, a Rococo style stucco ceiling inside and the doors leading to this room have remained of the original building. Everything else was replaced by a new building after 1969, when the city bought the derelict edifice.

In 1971, the Toy Museum (Spielzeugmuseum) opened its doors to the public and today, with its approximately 100,000 visitors per year, it ranks among the most sig-nificant of Nuremberg's numerous museums along with the German National Museum and the DB-Museum. It houses pictures, drawings and documents on the subject of "playing" and valuable toys, mostly from the 18th to 20th centuries, which are of cultural and historical interest. Legions of dolls with heads of wax, wood, papier mâché, porcelain, composition material, metal, biscuit porcelain and synthetics populate the exhibition rooms. They are dressed and barbered in the style of the time they were manufactured, mini-ature editions of the men and women of their age. The doll's houses, too, dis-play the same care for correct

A walk through the Toy Museum is an exciting experience for old and young visitors

historical detail, a meticulousness which also applies to the furniture within them, even to the smallest of appliances such as hot-water bottles or plates and jugs, shaving basins and the like. Shops, fairs and garden arbors all took form in the hands of skillful artisans just as all the numerous wooden figures which people the stalls and warehouses, castles and farmyards. Nuremberg's toymakers were especially inventive when it came to solving the problems of toy mobility with new drive systems or ways of moving them in a desired direction using clockwork, steam, gas and later, electrically driven means. More than a dozen local toy manufacturers took part in the development of model railways, steam engines and what later became known as the 'Meccano set' in English speaking countries. This museum displays, for example, a model railway which extends over an area of approximately 30 m^2 and which took 24 years to complete. It was made in Nuremberg and shows a railroad complex in the Mid-West of the USA. The list of objects exhibited in the museum includes irons and rocking horses, zinc and lead figures, clown and marionette dolls and a variety of metal toys and can be continued infinitely.

Varied and colorful as the collection is, it is matched by the regions from which the articles come. Along with Nuremberg we have the Thuringian Forest, Berchtesgaden, the Grödner Valley in South Tyrol, Oberammergau, and after 1750, the Erzgebirge region. Many of the exhibits, however, come from eastern European countries or even much further afield, or, simply, from the hands of a loving father who at one time presented his child with a new toy. For hundreds of years, Nuremberg has been known as the "World's Toy Center." There was no more suitable place to open a Toy Museum than right here in Nuremberg and thus add to the city's many attractions.

Toy Museum
Karlstr. 13–15, Tel. 09 11/2 31 31 64,
e-mail: museen@stadt.nuernberg.de,
Internet: www.museen.nuernberg.de,
open Tuesday to Sunday 10 a.m. –
5 p.m., Thursday 10 a.m. – 8 p.m.

6 St. Sebald's Church

Let us now turn to one of the two main places of worship within the city, **St. Sebald's Church**, situated in the center of the Sebalder Altstadt (St. Sebald's Quarter). The earlier building, the St.-Peters-Kapelle (St. Peter's Chapel), where the tomb of St. Sebald is presumed to have been located, is mentioned in the context of a pilgrimage in 1702. Since it is said that several healings occurred, Sebald was worshipped as saint of the people, but only canonized by the Pope in 1425.

Construction of the present-day church started about 1230 in the late Romanesque style. Parts of the transept and the eastern section of the choir were replaced between 1361 and 1379 by an imposing Gothic choir. Arched friezes mark the position of the original lower floors of the Romanesque west towers with their small window openings. The fourth upper floor was raised by Gothic masons in 1345 who made window apertures in the architectural style of their time. Finally, about 1483, a tall fifth floor with a belfry was added, in addition to the sound windows of varying height, the galleries as culmination and the 6th floor set further back with the pointed spire.

The Romanesque west choir soars up between the towers whose main section received three larger windows at the beginning of the 14th century. The central window is adorned with a crucifix cast in bronze by the metal-worker, Hans Wurzelbauer (1595–1656). In the area under the arch of the south portal, the Nuremberg sculptor, Adam Kraft (1455/60–1508) placed an artistic relief. It shows scenes from the legend of the Holy Cross.

We enter the church through the portal in the north tower with the relief by Heinz Heiber. The many church appointments were for the most part bequeathed by wealthy noble families here in Nuremberg. Passing under the Gothic west arcade, we enter the nave.

The epitaph appearing on the inner side of the left pillar is that of Ursula Holzschuher (d. 1504). Beneath the Coro-

*The tip of the "Beautiful Fountain" and the twin towers of
St. Sebald's Church*

nation of St. Mary we can see her first husband, Paulus Imhoff, her second husband, Nicolaus Tetzel, as well as the lady herself painted together with her five daughters. Opposite, on the triumphal arch of the west choir, a Gothic canopy crowns the stone statue of one of the Twelve Apostles (about 1340/50). The bronze font (about 1430) has an opening in its pedestal into which charcoal could be placed and ignited so as to warm the water in the upper portion. The 4 Evangelists carry the main body of the vessel while below, relief figures of apostles and saints decorate the pedestal.

We now follow the length of the Romanesque nave which already displays pointed arcades however. The open row of arcades above the string course forms a decorative motif which was frequently used in the Romanesque era. The walls end in the clerestory window where the open arcade rows and pillars lead through flower capitals to the ribbed vault. The angel's choir arches above the west choir. The artistic sandstone relief on the second pillar to the right was accomplished by Adam Kraft (1506) for the patrician, Peter Harsdörfer, showing Christ carrying the cross.

Further to the east we see that the aisles to the left and right are as high as the nave itself and constructed so as to round the choir. On a southern pillar of the east choir we find a memorial tablet for Carl III Holzschuher (1423–1480), a copy (middle of the 17th century) according to the original created by Albrecht Dürer about 1498/1500.

We can pause a moment here in the nave to have a look at one of the most interesting monuments the church has within its walls, namely, **St. Sebald´s Tomb**. We are speaking of the brass casing produced by Peter Vischer the Elder, standing 4.71 m high and which has been a worthy receptacle for the Gothic reliquary shrine (1391/97) of the church's patron saint since 1519. Four dolphins and twelve snails support the lower base. Over a base decorated with reliefs, a three-bay late Gothic canopy rises to accommodate the reliquary. A Renaissance style superstructure is placed over it. Peter Vischer has depicted himself – dressed in working attire – in a niche on the east side of the housing. At the corners of the base plate, we find

Tomb of St. Sebald´s by Peter Vischer the Elder and his sons (1507–1519) with the silver reliquary shrine (1391/97) containing the remains of the patron saint

four heroes of antiquity, and in front of the intermediate bases rest the female figures of the main virtues. In front of the pillars themselves on smaller columns stand the principal figures, the Twelve Apostles, which were cast using wax models. At the top of the construction, small-scale statues of the twelve prophets of the Old Testament are placed along with putti making music and dolphins. The inside of the protective housing of the shrine is of oak and carries the insignia of the empire and the city worked in silver. The beading is made of gold-plated copper. Inside rest the remains of St. Sebald.

The altar behind St. Sebald´s grave, seemingly pressed between the central columns of the aisle at the back of the choir, stands on the spot where the medieval altar once stood. An epitaph of the families Oelhafen-Pfinzing (1520–30) serves as retable depicting the Annunciation of Mary, with the donors kneeling below. A tapestry (about 1480) made of wool, silk and gold thread covers the sandstone table. The crucifixion group above the altar was produced by the famous wood carver, Veit Stoß (1447–1533). The figures of Mary and John as well as the crucifix itself once stood in the Frauenkirche (Church of Our Lady) and were reassembled in the church of St. Sebald as high altar in 1663.

Passing the pillar to the right of the altar, we come to the ambulatory. On the outer wall, we find a fresco (about 1386), which was carefully prised off the wall and placed in a frame at the beginning of the 20th century to save it from decay. It depicts Paul's disputes with the Jews (about 1390). The window above, called the Pfinzing Window, and the three windows following it are the work of Veit Hirsvogel (1461–1525) and are based on a design made by Albrecht Dürer.

The next window is an endowment made to the church by the Margrave von Brandenburg-Ansbach and was created according a design by Hans Süß von Kulmbach. In nine lines with a total height of 11 m, members of his family tree, saints and coats of arms of the counties under his protection are shown. The lower part of the window frames the commemorative donation of the churchwarden, Paulus Volckamer, and is a masterpiece from the hand of Veit Stoß. The reliefs show scenes from the Bible, among them, the Last Supper, Christ on the Mount of Olives and his arrest and are deeply chiseled from the sandstone. The date of this work, the master's symbol and a coded form of his name (in the upper part) are to be seen on the scabbard of a curved sword – 1499. This master mason's symbol is also to be found on the console of the statue of St. John and the date on the figure of St. Mary. Both these 2 m tall sculptures are carved from oak. In the lower corner of the relief one can see the donor family represented; to the left we find the father and his sons, to the right two women and two daughters.

The center window of the ambulatory flanked by the apostles, Peter and Paul, is a donation of Emperor Maximilian I, presumably according to a design by Albrecht Dürer. By the neighboring Bamberg Window, again according to a design by Albrecht Dürer, we discover a

left: Man of Sorrows (ca. 1390); center: Madonna with a radiant nimbus (ca. 1420); right: St. Sebald (ca. 1400)

niche for the sacraments (about 1370/80) framed by numerous statues. The fresco on the next wall area shows Hans Starck (d. 1473) as a pious worshipper. The window as well as those that follow it all go back to a time between 1380 and 1388, that is, the time when the choir was being completed. At that date, however, the windows were all filled with colored depictions of various kinds, but at the end of the 15th century the upper panes were replaced in the interests of better illumination and finally, in 1957, these in turn were replaced by smoked glass ones.

In the next but one wall area we find the memorial tablets for the patrician family of Tucher, without interruption from 1326 to the present day. In between there is a votive lamp from 1657. There are other donations from the Tucher family in the next space on the wall as well as on the pillar at the back. Here, we find an epitaph to Hans VI Tucher

(1426–1491), a painted representation of the stations of the cross decorated with many figures, a view of the city of Bamberg and portraits of the donor, his two wives, five sons and six daughters. As a continuation of memorial tablets of the Tucher family we find figures of St. John (about 1430 in clay) and the Apostle Andrew (about 1506), beautifully carved from lime-wood by Veit Stoß. Especially impressive is the presentation of the apostle's loosely falling curly hair, the cunningly-wrought folds of his garment, his attitude and the gesture adopted in pointing to the open book before him.

The adjoining three-sectioned tablet is also an endowment by the Tucher family, an epitaph dedicated to the provost, Dr. Lorenz Tucher (1447–1503). This triptych, in which the Italian influence is unmistakable, is said to be one of the main works created by the painter, Hans Süß von Kulmbach. One of the next pillars is embellished by the "Madonna with a radiant nimbus" (about 1425–30). It is the work of a Nuremberg master in the so-called "soft style" carved from pear-tree wood. The triumphal arch depicts the Last Judgment (1628), set within a memorial tablet and dedicated to the well-known collector of Dürer's work, Willibald I. Imhoff (1519–1580) and his ancestors. Beneath the main painting, we can see the name of the donor, Hans III Imhoff with eight of his ancestors, the famous Nuremberg legal scholar and humanist, Willibald Pirckheimer with his wife as well as the city's most well-known citizen, Albrecht Dürer.

The framed portrayal in the last section before coming to St. Mary's Portal served once as an antependium belonging to the altar of St. Peter. It shows St. Peter and also the donors, the family of Nicolaus Topler (d. 1487) with two wives, thirteen sons and seven daughters.

Open from:

March to May 9.30 a.m. – 6 p.m.,
June to August 9.30 a.m. – 8 p.m.,
September to December 9.30 a.m. –
6 p.m., January/February 9.30 a.m. – 4 p.m.

7 At the Fembohaus

As we leave St. Sebald´s Church, we turn left to Sebalder Platz and see the old **Sebalder Pfarrhof** (St. Sebaldus Rectory). Here we find a **"Chörlein"** (oriel altar niche) as it was originally intended – as house chapel. The masterful adjoining structure completed around 1370 has a richly decorated pillar and corpus with figure ornaments under the tracery windows. The original is kept in the German National Museum.

At Albrecht-Dürer-Platz, located a little bit higher, we find the great master, Nuremberg's most famous son, there to greet us, cast in bronze by Johann Daniel Burgschmiet in 1840 according to the design and model of Christian Daniel Rauch.

Across the square on the right we see the **Schürstabhaus**, an impressive, large patrician and burgher´s house which stands on basement vaults dating back to the 13th century. It belonged to the patrician family of Schürstab from 1328 to 1482, which explains the building's name. On the ground floor there is a chapel which was built around 1500 and can be admired through a glass door. Having suffered severe damage in the area of the roof during the war, the house was beautifully renovated in 1998.

At the eastern end of the church we discover Burgstraße climbing up towards a house that, even from this distance, is easily recognizable by its impressive gabled façade, and it may be that this house is the most well-preserved and most complete Renaissance style burgher's house in the whole city.

The **Fembohaus**, used as **City Museum** today, came into being from 1591–96 as the family residence of a merchant. It invites visitors to a trip through time covering 950 years of city history, starting with the "acoustic city model" from 1939 which can be found on the top floor. The floor situated below deals with subjects of city history, e.g. the Nuremberg Council, Nuremberg as Imperial City and Nuremberg as center of trade and handicrafts. Other rooms

Stadtmuseum Fembohaus

Burgstr. 15,
Tel. 09 11/2 31 25 95,
e-mail: museen@stadt.nuernberg.de,
Internet: www.museen.nuernberg.de

open from:
Tuesday to Sunday 10 a.m. – 5 p.m.,
Thursday 10 a.m. – 8 p.m.

impress the visitor by their valuable wall paneling and stucco ceilings, the paintings and wood carvings as well as their furniture from the 17th to 19th centuries. The multi-vision show "Noricama" presents a walk through Nuremberg's history and establishes contact with the famous inhabitants of this city.

The neighboring house made of stone, No. 17, displays a richly-decorated wooden oriel altar niche, typical of the Baroque era around 1700. A memorial table on house No. 21 commemorates the painter, Michael Wolgemut, Dürer's teacher, whose workshop and house used to be here. Albrecht Dürer's parents' house was located nearby where we now see the modern house on the corner of Obere Schmiedgasse. It belonged to his father, the gold-smith Albrecht Dürer the Elder. The famous painter lived in it until 1509, when he purchased what is nowadays cal-led the "Dürerhaus."

We walk along Burgstraße towards the east choir of St. Sebald's Church. Here we see an artistic relief, the **Schreyer-Landauersche Epitaph** (1490–92). It represents the oldest known work of the sculptor, Adam Kraft. From right to left it displays a populous series of scenes: Christ carrying the cross, Calvary's crosses, Christ being laid in his tomb and finally the resurrection of Christ. Below, we can see the numerous members of the donors' families. The relief in the middle shows the bearded faces of the donor, Sebald Schreyer, and the sculptor, Adam Kraft in the fore-ground on the right.

8 Around the Egidienkirche
(Extended Tour)

Theresienstraße leads from the north front of the Rathaus (City Hall), that is, the side facing the hills, and runs east to end in Theresienplatz. The **monument** erected in 1890 commemorates the Nuremberg citizen, **Martin Behaim**, seafarer, constructor and designer of the first globe (1491–92). The house on the opposite corner where Egidienplatz begins displays a statue of St. Sebald. To the right of this long-sided square we find a monument in stone (1826) to Philipp Melanchton. In 1526, he founded one of the first grammar schools in the city. House No. 13 has a memorial plaque for Anton Koberger (1440/45–1513) whose house and printing shop once stood here. He was one of the most important printers and book dealers of his time.

The square's centre boasts an **equestrian statue of Emperor Wilhelm I** and next to it rises the façade of the **Egidienkirche**. The original church in Romanesque style was burned to the ground in 1696. In the years 1711–18, the present church was erected in the simple, clear Baroque style. Only the two southern chapels survived the fire of 1696. The Romanesque **Eucharius Chapel** was built about 1120/30. The Gothic extension (ca. 1345) is a gift of the patrician family Tetzel and served as a memorial to the deceased members of that family. Adam Kraft created the memorial statuary representing the crowning of Mary, donated by Matthäus Landauer in 1503. The relief showing the crucifixion goes back to the years 1400/20.

St. Wolfgang´s Chapel (1437) links the twin chapels with the church. Along with a tastefully constructed late Gothic reticulated vault, it also possesses a stone relief showing the burial of Christ (about 1446). These buildings once belonged to the oldest of the nine monasteries in

Egidienkirche

open daily from 8 a.m. – 6 p.m., adjoining chapels by appointment. Tel. 09 11/2 14 11 41

Nuremberg, that of the Benedictine, St. Egidius, bestowed upon the community in 1140 by King Konrad III.

The upper side of Egidienplatz is bordered by a modern building. However, it contains parts of the once much-praised **Pellerhaus** which are worth seeing and which can be viewed during business hours. The building, erected between 1602 and 1607, was regarded at one time as Nuremberg's most splendid burgher´s house, but was almost completely destroyed in 1945. In the 1950's, the city restored the splendid hall, while the tower with the spiral staircase and the enchanting Renaissance courtyard were preserved and left standing as ruins. Strong pillars support the arches of the arcade which is crowned by a stone balustrade. In contrast, the archer decorating the **Apollo-brunnen** (Apollo Fountain) appears almost delicate. The

cast bronze figure was created in 1532 in the workshop of Pankraz Labenwolf, presumably according to a design by Peter Flötner and once adorned the courtyard of the Herrenschießerhaus am Sand.

Leaving the Pellerhaus we turn left and maintain this direction until we reach Hirschelgasse and find ourselves in front of the **Tucherschloss** (Tucher Castle) surrounded by extensive grounds. The oldest part of this building, which was restored in accordance with the original, was built in 1533–44 in the early Renaissance style. We can easily recognize this when we look at the attractive bay window facing the street and the elegant stair tower from the courtyard. The building serves as museum today. Unfortunately, the valuable fixed interior decoration, created mostly according to designs by Peter Flötner, was

*The Tucher Castle
from the courtyard
with stair tower*

destroyed during the war. The movable furniture was saved and gives us an idea of patrician wealth and splendor. The rich appointments – all loans by the Tucher family – consist of furniture, tapestries and paintings (among others by Wolgemut, Schäufelein, Neufchatel) and handicraft products, as e.g. magnificent wedding tableware by Wenzel Jamnitzer. The high-quality appointments give an insight into the way of life of Nuremberg patricians at that time.

In the garden, the **Hirsvogelsaal** (1534), the banquet hall of the estate of the Hirsvogel family, which was also destroyed during the war, was reconstructed because

the interior decoration (Peter Flötner) had been saved. The ceiling painting "The Fall of Phaeton" is the first of its kind north of the Alps, creating visual effects by illusory architecture and depth by foreshortening the lines. From the park we have a view of the modern university building.

Let us continue our way along Hirschelgasse and turn sharp right at its end to enter Äußere Laufer Gasse. Here we see one of the sturdy round towers of the city's fortifications, the

Georg Pencz created the ceiling painting for the Hirsvogelsaal (approx. 15 m long and 6 m wide). It represents "The Fall of Phaeton," a subject from Greek mythology

Museum Tucherschloss mit Hirsvogelsaal

Hirschelgasse 9 – 11,
Tel. 09 11/2 31 54 21,
e-mail: **museen@stadt.nuernberg.de,**
Internet: **www.museen.nuernberg.de,**

open **Monday 10 a.m. – 3 p.m.,**
Thursday 1 p.m. – 5 p.m., Sunday 10 a.m. – 5 p.m.

Laufer Torturm (Laufer Gate Tower). It once served to guard the road coming from Prague and Eger.

At the other end of this narrow street, the **Laufer-Schlagturm** marks the course of the city's fortifications before their last extension. This tower was erected in the 13th century, and only the uppermost floor with its spire were added after 1500.

Grübelstraße, which runs south in front of the Torturm (Gate Tower), shows us the course of the old city moat. The street is named after the Nuremberg town tiler and vernacular poet, Johann Konrad Grübel, (1736–1809) who is also commemorated by a plaque on House No. 8 as well as the Grübelsbrunnen (Grübel Fountain) at the Laufer-Schlagturm. Further down the street we find a section of the city's old moat still intact and this is the place where the crossbow archers used to practice.

It ends in the south with the Renaissance style **Schießhaus am Sand** (House of Archery), built in 1582/83. It is a very pleasant building with its decorative gabled front and the charming wooden oriel in the roof. The coats of arms above the door indicate that it is a municipal building, and it is still used for education purposes today. The attractive Apollo Fountain, now situated in the Pellerhaus, once stood in the courtyard of the Herrenschießhaus.

The eaves of the house facing south point the way into the city itself along Tucherstraße and its extension up to the northern section of the City Hall.

The City Hall

On the western side of the complex we find the broad and imposing **City Hall**, also referred to as the "Wolff'sche Rathaus." It was built in 1616–22 by the architect, Jakob Wolff the Younger, in the Italian Renaissance style. Six citizens' houses and one public building had to go to make room for this magnificent building, an edifice which is unique today among Germany's secular architecture. On the gable of the central portal we see the stone figures of Wisdom and Justice, between them a cartouche containing the bronze imperial eagle by Christoph Jamnitzer.

We pass beneath it into the impressive foyer – during office hours, of course – and discover the clear layout of columns and vaults. At the northern end of the hall we can admire excellent reproductions in gold of the imperial crown, imperial orb and scepter in memory of Emperor Sigismund who had the imperial insignia brought to Nuremberg in 1424 to be kept here forever.

The stairs on the opposite side lead us to the upper floor where the **"Große Rathaussaal"** (Great Council Chamber) is situated. It was built in 1332–40, has a length of 40 m, width of 12 m and a height of 12 m and was considered to be the largest pillar-free chamber north of the Alps. In 1520 the chamber was modernized under the supervision of Dürer. The wall paintings (according to his designs), glass paintings, paneling, a barrel vault and wall lights were combined to form a magnificent work of art in the Renaissance style.

Until 1806, this is where city council meetings took place as well as town trials, balls, the reception of emperors and princes, imperial assemblies and, in 1649, the signing of several peace treaties after the 30 Years' War occurred here. Unfortunately, the building, together with its irreplaceable treasures, was razed to the ground by fire in 1945. In 1956/58, the outer structure was rebuilt, followed by the reproduction of the barrel vault and the remaining wooden interior from 1980 on. In contrast, the smaller council chamber of the City Hall remained intact, but

East gable of the old Council Chamber with adjoining Beheim'scher Bau

cannot be visited. This room has a timbered ceiling (1620) which displays paintings by Paul Juvenell. In the central section we find a German emperor being showered with precious gifts by the Virtues. The smaller sections provided by the form of the ceiling show scenes from Roman history. On returning to the ground floor we take a look at the large City Hall courtyard with its pretty **Puttobrunnen** (Putto Fountain) (1557).

A narrow staircase leads down to the **Lochgefängnisse** (Dungeons) beneath the old Gothic City Hall. This was not a prison (the city towers no longer in use were available

Lochgefängnisse:
Sitzgruppe für Aufseher

for this purpose) but prisoners were kept here awaiting their trial. There is a guided tour for those who wish to take part. In the Middle Ages, conviction was only possible following a confession, therefore torture was considered to be a legitimate means to obtain a confession. The cells are furnished in the most primitive way. There are no articles of comfort except for a crudely carpentered wooden bench with a headrest, simple benches and a table, a hollowed-out stone for the reception of a clay vessel containing red-hot charcoal on cold winter days.

At the end of the corridor we go down several steps and thus reach the torture chamber. The hangman and his assistants had the job of extorting a confession from the accused in the presence of two councillor jurymen. For this operation 15th century Nuremberg judicial procedure allowed the following tools to be used:

1. Thumb and leg screws.
2. The "hoist." This involved tying the hands of the accused behind his back and lifting him into the air. Pain could be increased by attaching varying weights of stone or wood to the feet.
3. The rack. Here, the victim was tied to a ladder and stretched using a winch.
4. Placing the victim in a wooden "dish" lined with nails.
5. The burning of the skin with fire.

In 1532, Emperor Karl V restricted torture. In the 18th century, the Age of Enlightenment, it was only applied in a much more moderate form until it was abolished altogether in 1813. Apparently, certain cells were "reserved" for special criminals. Cell 11 shows a red rooster, the symbol for arson, the black cat over cell 12 indicates that slanderers were held prisoner here. In the two "stock" cells, the prisoners were unable to move at all.

At the next corner, the passageway branches and one way leads to three, walled-up cells. An underground waterway up to the bastions above by the Tiergärtnertor (Zoo Gate) and on to the narrower confines of the castle served as an escape route for the councillors. Again, unfortunately, it was destroyed by bombs in 1945. If we now proceed along a passage, through a large room and up a few steps we come to the prison smithy in which instruments of torture were fashioned. Next to it we see the supply chamber and kitchen of the "Lochwirt" (Warden of the Hole) who had to feed the prisoners. Finally, at the end of our route, we come upon the living quarters of the "Rathauswirt" (City Hall Host). This is certainly of more friendly aspect. The person who lived here had the job of looking after the prison complex, but also that of making sure that the councillors had enough to eat and drink during council meetings.

Historic Dungeons in the City Hall

**Tel. 09 11/2 31 26 90,
e-mail: museen@stadt.nuernberg.de,
Internet: www.museen.nuernberg.de,**

**open Tuesday to Sunday 10 a.m. – 4.30 p.m.,
closed on weekends from the middle of October
until the beginning of April. During the Christmas
Market opened daily**

Leaving the Rathaus now, we turn left and go down along the Rathaus. At the end of this splendid building we turn left again and end up in the courtyard of the new City Hall (1954–56). The center of attraction is a particularly charming **"Brunnen mit dem Gänsemännchen"** (Fountain with the Little Goose Man) as well as the Putto Fountain cast by Pankraz Labenwolf in the 16th century. Albrecht Dürer himself had already made a design for a well incorporating the popular legendary figure of the Little Goose Man as early as 1500. Behind this we notice the tall building of the **Oldest City Hall** (1332–40) whose Gothic tracery window on the first floor, that of the Great Council Chamber, reminds one of church architecture. The ground floor with the arcades used to accommodate shops. The gabled façade with the slender oriel and the pilaster strips rising higher than the roof are very attractive. Above the entry to the smaller City Hall courtyard, a narrow building has

"Fountain with the Little Goose Man" by Pankraz Labenwolf (mid-16th century)

squeezed itself in between its mighty neighbors. This is the so-called "Beheim'scher Bau" containing the "Kleine Ratsstube" (Little Councillors' Tavern). It is especially pleasing because of its richly decorated façade (1514/15).

10 The Hauptmarkt (Main Market) and the Schöner Brunnen (Beautiful Fountain)

A few steps now bring us to the main market square, the Hauptmarkt. During the time immediately before Christmas, Germany's most famous Christmas Market, the 'Christkindlesmarkt' is held here. In 1349, Emperor Karl IV supported the city council in its request to establish a market place between the Sebaldus District and what was to become the Lorenzer District in the south instead of the Jewish quarter that existed there. At the same time, Nuremberg's inhabitants availed themselves of the opportunity to get rid of their unpopular fellow citizens. Ulman Stromer gave an account on the events of December 5, 1349 from his own experience in a book written around 1390, stating that the Jews had been burnt. 562 of the about 1500 inhabitants of the Jewish quarter fell victim to the pogrom. The large square surrounded by walls has since then served as market and meeting point for tourists, as a place for showing reverence, holding feasts and tournaments. In addition, the imperial insignia, revered like a saint's relies, were shown to the religious population here each year until the Reformation.

Above a low octagonal water basin, the four-step stone pyramid of the **Schöner Brunnen** (Beautiful Fountain) rises 17.30 m high. It numbers among the oldest pipe-fed fountains in the city and has possessed its own direct supply since its construction between 1395 and 1396. The master who built it was presumably Heinrich Beheim from the Parler family. Forty stone figures at four levels supplement the richly-ornamented design. The bottom row shows the seven free arts together with Philosophy; a little higher behind these we can see the four Evangelists and the four Church Fathers. The central row consists of the seven Electors and three heroes from classical antiquity (Hector, Alexander and Caesar), three from the Old Testament (Joshua, David, Judas Maccabeus) and three occidental heroes, (King Arthur, Charlemagne, Godfrey of Bouillon). At the very top we see Moses and seven Old Testament prophets. Today's well is a reproduction (about 1900) made of shell lime. Fragments of the weather-beaten original consisting of sandstone are exhibited in the German National Museum. The finely-wrought ironwork around the well was constructed by Paulus Kuhn in 1587. In the southeast part we find a gold-colored ring worked into the upper part of the wrought iron and which is moveable. To everyone's astonishment, there is not a joint or seam to be found on the ring. This so-called "Wishing Ring," so legend has it, was incorporated into the work by an apprentice without his master's knowledge. Formerly, it was regarded as one of Nuremberg's landmarks, and many a legend has been spun, as the ring supposedly fulfills your wishes when you turn it.

The main market with fruit and vegetable stalls; behind, the Frauenkirche

Schöner
Brunnen

11 The Frauenkirche (Church of Our Lady)

The Frauenkirche which towers above the Market Square can perhaps be looked upon as a symbol of atonement for the destruction of the Jewish quarter. Emperor Karl IV who, in 1349, had given his consent to the deed, bestowed the church on his favorite city with the words: "For the glory of the empire, the honor of the Mother of God and salvation of the dead." The church was erected be-

The artistic clock (1509) on the Frauenkirche shows the pageant, the "Männleinlaufen", every day at noon

tween 1350 and 1358. As master mason, the emperor chose the Swabian, Peter Parler (about 1330–1399) who had been active in the construction of Prague Cathedral.

Typical of the most successful son of a family of architects and masons is his richly tessellated and ornamented façade. Together with the side walls, this is the only part of the building which survived the air raids of 1945 intact. This place of worship was a Protestant church from the Reformation (1525) in Nuremberg on. When Nuremberg became part of Bavaria, most of the valuable interior appointments were removed. In 1816, the church was given to the Catholics. It received new fittings, for the most part from the secularized Nuremberg monastery churches.

The western façade is dedicated to the honor of Mary, who is enthroned in the middle of the double portal, surrounded by saints, patriarchs and prophets. The parapet with its tracery work decorated with coats of arms above was once the place from which the imperial insignia, the crown, scepter and orb, sword and holy lance were shown to the public on the occasion of the baptism of the successor to the throne, Wenzel, in 1361. The imperial insignia are kept in the Hofburg in Vienna today. The gable of St. Michael's choir to be seen behind the parapet is the work of Adam Kraft from 1506–08. The clock situated on the gable, which was manufactured in 1509, daily brings forth its little pageant at noon called **"Männleinlaufen."** Upon a signal given by the trumpeter standing to one side, seven electors dressed in red pay homage to Emperor Karl IV by walking round him three times. The scene recalls the imperial law passed in Nuremberg in 1356, the Golden Bull, which decreed that the seven electors, the archbishops of Mainz, Cologne and Trier, the king of Bohemia, the Palatine count at the Rhine, the Duke of Saxony and the Margrave of Brandenburg were each to elect the new king and that the latter was to hold his first Reichstag (imperial diet) in the city of Nuremberg.

Now we enter the oldest hall church in Franconia. The wall paintings in the vestibule go back to the year 1880 while the statues stem from the 14th century. The boss in the vaulting of the vestibule shows the crowning of the Virgin Mary. Entering the church's main nave, our eyes are not so much directed upward as is the case in Gothic church planning, but rather take in the spaciousness of the area, and the effect is a calming one. The central aisle leads us

Madonna of the Radiant Nimbus on the windowsill of the central choir window (ca. 1440)

to two paintings executed on the first two round columns. The left (about 1440) depicts the resurrection of Christ, while the right one shows St. Michael as a slayer of dragons and a weigher of souls. The painting on the wall facing us shows a Holy Family scene, portrayed around the year 1520, and next to this there is an altar displaying a late Gothic Madonna (about 1480). The Madonna of the Radiant Nimbus (about 1440) to be seen in the center choir window originates, like the Angel of the Annunciation on the right wall of the choir and the group signifying the Annunciation opposite, come from the Welser Altar whose figures were sold individually in 1815. The choir's boss is probably unique; it shows the young Jesus going to school.

Standing in the east choir we look over and upward to the gallery to the symbolic place where the emperor had his seat. Artistic tracery adorns the parapet and vault. Representations of the crucifixion and Christ being buried are relics from altars dating back to about 1500. To the left as we pass from the nave to the east choir we come across one of the two masterpieces executed by Adam Kraft and which are exhibited in this church. It is the colored epitaph of Hans Rebeck showing the crowning of Mary which was initially located in the Dominican Church. It represents the Coronation of the Virgin Mary.

The Tucher Altar (about 1440/50) in the choir apse once served as high altar in the Augustinian Church of St. Veit. The paintings on the altar panels are said to be the most important work representative of the pre-Dürer epoch. The stout, realistic figures depict St. Monica with her son Augustine, the Annunciation, Crucifixion and Resurrec-

The choir apse of the Frauenkirche with the so-called Tucher Altar (1445)

tion as well the hermits, Paul and Antony. An outstanding memorial table is the so-called Peringsdörffsche Epitaph (about 1498) on the north side wall, also a work by Adam Kraft. In the center we see the Madonna in a protective cloak, adored by the pope, the emperor, bishops, citizens, soldiers and peasants.

Frauenkirche

Open:
Mon. – Sat. 9 a.m. – 6 p.m.; Sun. and public holidays 12.30 – 6 p.m. Daily at noon the "Männleinlaufen" of the clock where figures appear, Emperor Karl IV and the 7 Electors.

12

At the Heilig-Geist-Spital (Holy Ghost Hospital)

The Hauptmarkt slopes gently towards the south. We will walk in this direction until we reach the Museumsbrücke (Museum Bridge). From this position we can enjoy one of the most beautiful subjects adopted by painters, photographers and the designers of "Lebkuchen" (gingerbread) tins, the northern section of the Pegnitz River with the Holy

View towards the Holy Ghost Hospital with night-illumination

Ghost Hospital. The central pillar supporting the double arch has its continuation in an oriel which is decorated with coats of arms and whose pointed top reaches the height of the steep gabled roof. From this point we go around the hospital building located to our left and walk along its north front until the street widens into Hans-Sachs-Platz.

In 1874, a **monument** was erected here to the most famous poet of the 16th century, **Hans Sachs** (1494–1576). He belonged to the Nürnberger Meistersinger, but also managed to make himself immortal as a "shoemaker poet," having composed more than 4000 songs, about 2000 poems, 120 tragedies and comedies and 85 carnival plays. At the end of the hospital we turn right and go over the Spitalbrücke (Hospital Bridge) to the island "Schütt."

Stone crucifix by Adam Kraft in the Crucifixion Court

From here we reach one of the courtyards of the hospital, surrounded by several smaller buildings. This important social institution characterizing the medieval town was donated to the city by the wealthy city mayor, Konrad Groß, in 1339. As a result of numerous other donations and gifts, an extension was necessary around 1500 and therefore the Pegnitz was built over (1511–27, Hans Beheim the Elder). Today, as in the past, this building is used primarily as accommodation for the aged. A double stairway leads to what is known as Crucifixion Court with its notable cloisters. The long side of the courtyard has wooden, covered walkways borne on strong-looking, round columns and firm supporting arches. On the north side there is an impressively designed **Crucifixion Group**, also made by Adam Kraft and originally meant for St. John's Cemetery. To the right the belfry tower of the Spitalkirche (Hospital Church) looms above. It was here that the imperial insignia were kept between 1424 and 1796. In the northern part of the courtyard, in the so-called "Hanselhof" stands a replica of the **Hanselbrunnen** (Hansel Fountain), the original of which is kept in the German National Museum. It was created in 1380 as one of Nuremberg's oldest bronze hollow castings and shows a schawm-player.

We leave the hospital the way we came in. Opposite we see the Schuldturm (Debtors' Tower), built in about 1323. It is one the last remains of the penultimate city fortification and was used to imprison those who did not pay their debts from 1478 on. The Heubrücke (Hay Bridge) leads us back to the "mainland" south of the Pegnitz.

13

At the Katharinenkirche
(Church of St. Catherine)

At this point we first follow the course of Peter-Vischer-Straße, bearing to the left pursuing the same way that the old city wall takes. Immediately behind a picturesque, half-timbered house, one catches a glimpse through an arched gateway of the courtyard once belonging to a Dominican monastery dissolved in the 16ᵗʰ century. The **St. Katharina-Kirche** (Church of St. Catherine) was founded in the late 13ᵗʰ century and served as a meeting place for the famous Nürnberger Meistersinger from 1620 until 1778. In 1945, it was burned down and only its side walls were left standing. The ruin has been preserved in more or less this condition and today is used as a backdrop for various musical and theater events.

Across the church ruin, we see the Music University. Taking the next lane left, we reach the "CINECITTA," a multiplex cinema opened in 1995 and an IMAX cinema which was inaugurated in 2001.

The next open space we come to reveals the large proportions of the new Baroque Bavarian State Chamber of Commerce (Landes-Gerwerbeanstalt). It was built 1892–97 according to the plans of Theodor von Kramer and accommodates the collection of the "Bayerisches Gewerbemuseum" (Bavarian Trade Museum) founded in 1869. Owing to increased technical requirements and greater demand for space, the building was sold to the "Nürnberger Versicherung" insurance company in 1989 and has been meticulously renovated. Since then, the building has been used for education purpose by the Nürnberger Akademie für Versicherungswirtschaft (Nuremberg Insurance Business Academy) on the one hand, and by the Education Center of the city of Nuremberg on the other.

In the nearby modern "Norishalle," which was built in 1965–69, we find the Museum of the Natural History Society and the City Archive. For our part, however, we now turn right just before the main street and walk down the lane called "Marientormauer" (Mary's Gate

Wall) which runs along the inside of the former city wall. At the point where we cross Lorenzer Straße we find the **Kunsthalle** (Art Gallery) at the Marientor. International contemporary art is presented here. We continue our tour along this lane which now changes its name to "Königstormauer" (King's Gate Wall). The **Baumeisterhaus**, standing on its own, with its colored coats of arms, forms the end of the lane. The house is the work of master Jakob Wolff the Younger who built the sturdy building at the behest of the city council in 1615 as an official residence for the town's master builder. A year later, he began the immense task of constructing the new City Hall. A table on the adjoining buildings reminds us of the former polytechnic institute (1829) where the famous physicist Georg Simon Ohm held his lectures.

The "Baumeisterhaus" by Jakob Wolff the Younger served as official residence for the town's master builder (1615)

14 At the Königstor (King's Gate)

On the opposite side of busy Königstraße (King Street) we catch sight of one of Nuremberg's landmarks, the round **Frauentorturm** (Women's Gate Tower). This edifice is about 40 meters high, it was built in 1388 – at that time square and not round – and guarded one of the city's five gates. These towers, with the exception of the Tiergärtnertor, were encased in broad, round, stone walling between 1556 and 1559. Their diameter thus increased to a total of 18 m, the wall was 7 m thick.

The gate towers were a central part of the city's fortification, an impressive protective barrier of some five kilometers length. It consisted of the main wall (7 – 8.50 m high, 1 m thick) with a sentry-walk, the 15 m wide keep, the outer wall and the 20 m wide and up to 12 m deep moat. The city council had this enormous stronghold reinforced at the gates by drawbridges and bastions, as had been done at the Frauentorturm. This stronghold was thus never conquered by an enemy in all the centuries.

Wooden bridge leading to the Frauentor, which we pass to reach the Tradesmen's Court

In the Waffenhof (Gun Yard) next to the Königstor we come across the **Handwerkerhof** (Artisans' Court) "Alt Nürnberg" a quarter very well-suited to exemplify a typical medieval tradesmen's lane and it is here that the past becomes a living experience. The visitor is invited for a stroll, to look and buy the excellent artisan's products.

Leaving the Handwerkerhof through the western gate in the direction of the city center, we come to the newly created Klarissenplatz.

Handwerkerhof

Tel. 09 11/8 60 70,
e-mail: info@handwerkerhof.de,
Internet: www.handwerkerhof.de
Open: March 20 till Christmas 10 a.m. –
6.30 p.m., Sunday and public holidays closed.
Restaurants open 10.30 a.m. – 10 p.m.

On the west side of this square, we see the **Neues Museum Nürnberg** (New Museum Nuremberg), which exhibits international contemporary art and design. This museum has a fascinating external appearance owing to the impressive architecture of Volker Staab. The curved glass façade creates an impression of lightness, it allows you to look into the exhibition rooms on the one hand, and creates fascinating reflections on the other.

Neues Museum Nürnberg,

**Klarissenplatz/
Luitpoldstr. 5,
Tel. 09 11/ 2 40 20-0,
e-mail: info@nmn.de,
Internet: www.nmn.de,**

**open Tuesday to Friday 10 a.m. – 8 p.m.,
Saturday/Sunday 10 a.m. – 6 p.m.**

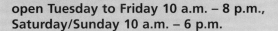

We now proceed along Königstraße in the direction of the Old Town center. Looking through a building-site gap, we catch a glimpse of the **St. Martha-Kirche** (St. Martha's Church) which was built for the pilgrim's hospital founded in 1363 and consecrated in 1385. After the Reformation, the church served as domicile for the Meistersinger from 1578 until 1620. With the windows donated around 1390, this church has one of the earliest stained-glass cycles of Nuremberg.

On the opposite side of the street we notice the **St. Klara-Kirche** (St. Clara's Church), an even older church, consecrated in 1273. The extensions carried out from 1428 until 1458 resulted in an increased height of the church and the women's choir, plus additional windows, an oratory and a new vestry. The church served as monastery church of the Sisters of St. Clare. The grave of the abbess, Caritas Pirckheimer (d. 1532), was found near the façade in 1959. She was the sister of the renowned humanist, Willibald Pirckheimer. In front of the church stands a bronze sculpture by Gerhard Marcks.

The Mauthalle and Zeughaus (Customs Hall and Arsenal)

Having arrived at Hallplatz, we find ourselves standing opposite the substantial building of the **Mauthalle** (Customs Hall) in which the imperial city customs office (Maut = customs) had its headquarters after 1572. It is one of three corn houses which were erected by Hans Beheim the Elder around 1500 at the request of the city council. This massive building was built into the penultimate city moat. It consists mainly of a great number of large cellars whose pillars carry two main floors. All of this is enclosed by a six-story roof with innumerable hatches and windows.

Opposite its west gable on the other side of the building, there is a square building dating back to 1588. This building façade is all that is left of the former **Zeughaus** (Arsenal) of the imperial city. Two sturdy round domed towers flank the portal of this Renaissance structure which accommodates a police station today.

Gate decorated with coats of arms (1588) of the former arsenal of the imperial city

The Germanisches Nationalmuseum (German National Museum) (Extended Tour)

If we now proceed along the same side as the gable of this building, the **German National Museum** appears after about 100 meters, occupying a whole block between Korn-markt and the city wall. The main entrance has been situa-ted in the Kartäusergasse since completion of the exten-sion building in 1993. The lane was designed by the Israeli artist Dani Karavan as a "Way of Human Rights". The round pillars made of white concrete are engraved with the articles of the human rights in German and in various languages as a symbol of international understanding.

The nucleus of the complex is the former **Carthusian monastery** with its church (1381–83), and cloisters

left:
View into Kartäusergasse, designed by Dani Karavan as a "Way of Human Rights"

right:
Round pillars, each showing one article of the General Declaration of Human Rights each

(15th century), put at the museum's disposal in 1857. Parts of the former Augustinian monastery were transferred here but were destroyed in World War II. This was the fate of most historical buildings erected in the 19th century, so that many of the museum's buildings were constructed after 1955.

Today, the biggest museum of German art and cultural history comprises a total exhibition space of 28,000 sqm. Those wishing to visit it are therefore recommended to reserve several hours for the purpose. About 300,000 visitors come to see the museum each year. From prehistoric times, weapons and ceramic objects (mostly found in tombs) bear witness to man's way of life then. These are supplemented by individual items such as the richly ornamented gold cone found at Ezelsdorf (12th–11th century B.C.) weighing 310 g. The exhibition of treasures and works of art is continued on the ground floor and spans a period of time ranging from the Carolingians up to the end of the Middle Ages. The floor above is reserved for painting, sculptures and objects of art from modern times which presents the development of artistic styles without interruption from Dürer's time to the present day. From the very beginning, the museum did not only collect clothes, furniture and jewelry of the ruling classes of an epoch, but also toys, baking forms and the chests of ordinary folk, Jewish antiques and festive apparel from all German-speaking regions. Among these collector's items were objects of popular piety as much as those reflecting humanistic convictions, furnishings from medieval churches, stone garden sculptures of the Rococo period and objects demonstrating the art of the German gold-smith. There are special collections which mark the course of cultural history to be seen from the assembled pieces. The section dealing with musical instruments, for example, which also happens to be the largest collection of pianos in the world, is evidence of this development. The museum also houses the largest library (about 570,000 volumes) on German cultural history as well as a comprehensive collection of drawings. A special attraction here is the first preserved **globe**, manufactured by **Martin Behaim** in Nürnberg during 1491–92 – omitting, of course, the Americas. Among the most valuable pieces exhibited are sketches, drawings and paintings by **Albrecht Dürer** and also numerous carvings by the sculptor, **Veit Stoß**.

The museum was founded in 1852 by the Association of German Researchers into History and Antiquity on the initiative of the Franconian baron, Freiherr Hans von und zu Aufsess, who was in charge of its management in the early years of development. The purpose was to support the nation in its efforts for political unity by creating an awareness for the common past. Thus, the founding of the "Germanisches Nationalmuseum" provided a place of mutual identity to the German-speaking world which was supported by the entire population and did not take into account political frontiers. The cost of the museum's up-keep is borne jointly by the city, the state of Bavaria and the federal government but the new works of art are even today acquired through contributions and donations of the members and supporters in the spirit of the foundation rules from 1852.

Germanisches Nationalmuseum

Kartäusergasse 1,
Tel. 09 11/1 33 10,
e-mail: info@gnm.de,
Internet: www.gnm.de,

open Tuesday to Sunday 10 a.m. – 6 p.m.,
Wednesday 10 a.m. – 9 p.m.

17

The St. Lorenzkirche (St. Lawrence´s Church)

There is a shop-lined street which passes between the Mauthalle and the Zeughaus called Pfannenschmiedgasse (Tinsmith Alley) and which leads directly to the **St. Lorenzkirche**. This church strongly resembles its sister church, St. Sebald´s Church, both from its external appearance and as far as the quality of its interior furnishings is concerned.

The present building was begun in 1260 on the foundations of an earlier, smaller Romanesque basilica with three aisles and ended a hundred years later when the tracery work of the rose window with its many levels and 10.28 m outside diameter and 5.90 m inner diameter was set on the decorative wall between the church's twin towers. At the end of the 14th century, the outer walls were placed at the very end of the buttresses in order to gain space for chapels and larger windows. In the meantime, the settlements north and south of the river Pegnitz had become united under the encircling protection of one city wall, and more and more wealthy families moved to the Lorenzer section of the city. In this way, more money flowed into the church coffers and donations contributed to the rich furnishings of the church itself.

In order to compete with St. Sebald across the river, this church had a silver shrine constructed, similar to that designed for St. Sebaldus' tomb and intended for the mortal remains of Saint Deocarus, Charlemagne's confessor. As a result of the workship of St. Deocarus – or the altar of the Twelve Apostles (1437) – there was a need to build a choir with an ambulatory round the back of the altar such as St. Sebald possessed. With the participation of several master masons, the work was completed in 38 years (1439–77). This is all the more surprising in view of the fact that the city council had ordered that only money collected from public donations be used for the modification. Despite the Reformation and subsequent war, most of the priceless treasures remained intact. Severe losses were suffered only following the incorporation of the city into Bavaria (1806). To reduce the city's debts, irreplaceable works such as the silver coffin of St. Deocarus and the

medieval bronze baptismal font were sold – both were subsequently melted down.

During World War II the transportable church furnishings were stored in the so-called art bunker (rock cellar under the castle), but the building itself was severely damaged. The vault of the nave was destroyed from the clerestory window on, while the vault of the east chancel was greatly damaged but did not collapse. The two towers and the western façade as well as the surrounding walls remained intact. However, the Nuremberg citizens and the parishioners of St. Lawrence succeeded in raising the funds, even though times were difficult, to rebuild their church, so that it was used again as early as 1952.

The picture story in the arch of the **main door** represents one of the most precious works in sculpture: depictions of the life of Christ and, above these, the Passion, lead to the Last Judgment, God the Father gathers the blessed on his right and on his left the damned, who descend into hell. Above all this Christ as Judge of the World, assisted by Mary and John the Baptist. The narrative is framed by 14 prophets and the 12 apostles, supplemented in the lower part by the figures of Adam and Eve – symbols of the original sin – two more prophets and the church patrons Lawrence and Stephen. The multitude of figures making up the composition, the portal, the rose and the 12 meter-high decorative gable and their similarity to the west façade of the Frauenkirche and numerous French cathedrals shows the strong influence of the Parler family in church planning.

The lantern cupola of the north tower was replaced by a steel construction after it was struck by lightning, which makes it look different from its southern counterpart. At the foot of the tower we see an iron measuring tape, determining how long 6 "Nuremberg working shoes" (27.84 cm each = 167.04 cm) is.

Entering the church through the southern side entrance (apothecary's door) we walk to the center aisle and let the harmony of the church take its effect. The smiling Adoration Madonna (about 1285) situated on the fourth northern column is among the oldest sculptures Nuremberg possesses. A little further on, we find the late-Gothic, **bronze candelabrum** (1489) by Peter Vischer. The suspension fitting in the vaulted ceiling was a technical masterpiece. The archangel Michael carved in wood (before 1477) may be an early work of art by Veit Stoß. On the right-hand pillar, a group of three figures (about 1490) portrays the martyrdom of St. Sebastian, the patron saint guarding against the plague. This contagion was a terrible scourge for the local population from the 14th century until its last appearance in 1713. The last column pair in the nave is decorated by the framed wooden figures of the two church patrons, Lawrence (left) and Stephen (1440/50). The modern altar at the end of the nave is flanked by the altar of St. Catherine (1485/90), the work of Michael Wolgemut, and to the left the altar of St. Nicholas (1505/10). The altar panels are painted by Hans Süß von Kulmbach, one of Dürer's pupils.

*above: St. Catherine's Altar from the Wolgemut workshop with altar panels painted by the master himself (1485/90). On the pillar of the side aisle, St. Stephen as deacon, whose attributes are lost. **right**: Representation of the Annunciation by Veit Stoß, the so-called Angel's Greeting (1517)*

The transition from the nave to the chancel is marked in particular by the Triumphal Cross with a larger than life-size crucifix (end of the 14th century), an endowment by the Imhoff family.

Three works of art dominate the inner chancel: the tabernacle, a gilded candelabrum and especially the **"Engelsgruß"** (Angel´s Greeting), a major work of the famous artist, Veit Stoß. Both works of art were commissioned by the "Vorderster Losunger" (Lord Mayor) Anton Tucher II in 1517/1518 for a total of 550 guilders, including installation.

The candelabrum which has an approximate diameter and height of 2.5 meters is made of gilded iron and supports fifty-five candle holders of gilded wood. The statue in the upper section represents the crowned Mary, a creation from the workshop of Veit Stoß.

The main figures of the "Engelsgruß" are Gabriel, the angel of the Annunciation, and the Virgin Mary, looking

Reverse side of the "Angel´s Greeting" with sun medallion

Reverse side of the "Angel's Greeting" with moon medallion

at the same time submissive and dismayed. The wreath incorporates 55 roses, the same number as candles on the candelabrum. They symbolize the rosary devotions: five times ten "Hail Mary" each followed by an "Our Father." Angelic figures fly about the main personages, and God the Father is placed above them all.

The modern altar is adorned with a crucifix conceived by Veit Stoß, probably between 1516 and 1520. The head, body and loincloth are carved from a single piece of lime-wood.

The structure of the **tabernacle** soars almost 20 meters to the vault like a climbing plant. The numerous figures and scenes between the pinnacles narrate the story of the Passion, as agreed upon in the contract signed with the donor Hans Imhoff. We pass between the tabernacle and the commemorative plaque to the American, Rush Kress, patron of the arts and benefactor during the period of re-establishment after World War II, and descendant of

View into the east choir of St. Lawrence´s Church with its outstanding works of art

one of the distinguished families in the town, Kress von Kressenstein, and reach the ambulatory. The left altar of the three standing here next to each other is the **Deocarus Altar** (1437). It housed the silver shrine until 1811 when it was sold and thrown in the melting pot. The holy relics have been kept at Eichstätt since 1845. The paintings, effected on a gold background, show the taking of the confession of Charlemagne and the death of his confessor on the left while, on the right, Emperor Ludwig the Bavarian hands to the Nuremberg clergy the relics which were revered here.

The window glazing above the choir, the Imperial Window (1477), originates from Hans Wolgemut's workshop.

It was donated by Emperor Friedrich III and his wife, Eleonora of Portugal. Beneath it stands the Krell Altar (about 1483). The background of the painting is especially interesting as it shows the oldest depiction of the city of Nuremberg. The second window to the right of this, the splendidly colorful Volckamer Window, was created in Strasbourg around 1480 and is considered to be a master-piece of late Gothic stained glass work. A very large in-scription on the front wall of this aisle shows the date 1477 when the work on the choir was completed.

We start our tour of the church's side aisles with the St. Roche Altar. The altar was donated to the church by the Imhoff family around 1483/85, a time when the plague was raging in Nuremberg. The expressive main figures depict Saint Roche showing his plague swellings to an angel. A stone relief follows (about 1500) which portrays the strangling of Beatrix, another work by Adam Kraft. The figures of the Virgin Mary, St. Anthony, the bishops and St. Veronica are creations from the late 14th century. Dürer's pupil, Hans Süß von Kulmbach, signed the two wing paintings of the adjoining St. Anne's Altar (1523).

The last window in this aisle was manufactured by Veit Hirsvogel after a motif conceived by Dürer. The Feyer-glocke (Feyer Bell) beneath the organ gallery was made in the early 14th century, but had to be removed after heavy artillery fire had damaged it in the last war.

Passing the first south pillar of the side aisle, where we can see a picture of the destroyed St. Lawrence´s Church, we leave this second largest Nuremberg church and its art treasures collected by pious citizens to enrich their place of worship.

St.-Lorenzkirche

Open:
Monday to Saturday 9 a.m – 5 p.m.,
Sunday 1 – 4 p.m., mass every
workday at 5 p.m.

The Tugendbrunnen (Fountain of Virtue) and Nassauer Haus

The Tugendbrunnen (Fountain of Virtue), located north of the western façade of St. Lawrence's Church is one of the city's landmarks. The bronze column rises from an octagonal basin, it has three levels and is adorned with seven human figures.

These female figures represent the seven Virtues of the Middle Ages, identifiable by the typical attributes: Faith (cross), Love (children), Hope (anchor), Magnanimity (lion), Moderation (jug and vessel), Patience (lamb) and, crowning the spring's column, Justice (eyes bound with scales and sword).

The putto figures on the central level bear the imperial city's insignia. Powerful water jets stream out of their trumpets as well as from the breasts of the female figures, so that an apparently disordered criss-crossing of water jets ensues. The fountain dates back to 1584–1589

left:
The Fountain of Virtue (1584–89) by Benedikt Wurzelbauer showing the seven main Virtues

right:
The so-called Nassau House, the only preserved medieval residential tower in Nuremberg

and is the work of the brass-founder, Benedikt Wurzel-bauer, symbolising the sensual gaiety of the Renaissance.

Exactly opposite, we discover the six-story **Nassauer Haus** (Nassau House). This form of Romanesque residential tower as a place to live for the gentry was quite common up to the 13th century in Germany. Built originally as a residence for estate officials, it is the only preserved example of a tower house in Nuremberg.

This is, in fact, the oldest residential building in Nuremberg, at least as far as the cellar and the next two upper floors are concerned. Among the many owners of the house, it is mentioned that Jobst Haug added many features of the house in 1421–23. The two upper floors from the 15th century with their regular brickwork differ clearly from the older floors below where irregular stones were used. In 1427, Ulrich Ortlieb purchased the building.

He had the top floor with the coat of arms and corner oriels built in 1433. This must have been the time when the altar niche was added to the east side. It is said that the rich citizen, Ulrich Ortlieb, granted King Sigismund a loan of 1,500 guilders in 1431 and was given a crown as collateral.

The insignia on the stone balustrade bear witness to this event and were placed there by this proud lender of money: Archduchy of Austria, large coat of arms of the city of Nuremberg, Earldom of Cilly, Trier, Cologne, Mainz, coat of arms of the Roman king, of Pope Eugenius IV, of the Holy See (key), of the city of Rome (S.P.Q.R.) and of the Roman emperor, the coat of arms of Bohemia, the Electorate of the Palatine, Saxony, Brandenburg, St. Lawrence, the small coat of arms of the city of Nuremberg, Ortlieb.

The name of the house, however, is a misnomer. In later years, the affair of the pawned crown was falsely attributed to King Adolf of Nassau (1292–98).

The building, as a last relic of a past architectural era, has belonged to the Schlüsselfeld family foundation since 1709.

The Weißer Turm (White Tower)

Karolinenstraße leads from the Nassauer Haus building westwards. At Hefnerplatz we come across a bronze statue at the **Peter-Henlein-Brunnen** (Peter Henlein Fountain), the Nuremberg mechanic, (1485–1542) who was for a long time regarded as the inventor of the pocket watch. At any rate, he was among the first to manufacture a spring-operated watch. We see him holding one of the early pocket watches, the "Nuremberg egg" while his foot rests upon a clock weight.

Ludwigsplatz begins at a modern water spring and shortly afterwards we find ourselves face to face with the **Weißer Turm** (White Tower). It was one of the gate towers of the older town fortification (middle of the 13th century) and today stands above the station of an underground railway. The side facing the city is adorned with three coats of arms: the two of Nuremberg, and above them the imperial eagle held by two lions. Before we pass through the gate, let us take a look at the richly figured, modern fountain in front of us, the so-called **"Ehekarussel"**

The "Marriage Carousel," created by von Jürgen Weber (1984) according to a poem by Hans Sachs: The bitter-sweet conjugal life

Figure of the young loved one on the fountain called the "Marriage Carousel"

(Marriage Carousel). What seems to be confusing at first sight is resolved by looking at the poem composed by Hans Sachs in 1541. Human beings and animals depict scenes which drastically represent the good, but also the bad sides of conjugal life (created by Prof. Jürgen Weber, Braunschweig, 1984).

The impregnability of this White Tower was substantially enhanced by the city's masons by the addition of a small bastion with round towers and an outer gate. We cross Dr.-Kurt-Schuhmacher-Straße which follows the course of the older city moat.

At the Jakobskirche (St. James' Church)

Jakobsplatz is dominated by the **churches of St. James** (to the left) and **St. Elisabeth**. The latter was the house chapel of the German Order of Teutonic Knights upon whom this parcel of land, which had been the old royal courtyard, was bestowed by Emperor Otto IV as a gift in 1209, and which later supported the oldest hospital in the town.

However, the official church of the Order was **St. Jakob** (St. James). The elongated choir of today's building stems from the middle of the 14th century, the nave from the 15th century. This house of worship with its pointed towers has been brilliantly restored after the damage it received in 1945 and today has many treasures worth seeing once again. Among them are the sandstone figures to be found in the choir (14th century) and the four figures of the apostles made from clay (1410/20) which are all older than the building itself, as well as the tabernacle which was produced at the same time as the interior of the choir.

This main altar (about 1370) is said to be the oldest shrine altar in the city. The Gothic decorative gable and the figures painted on a golden background on the altar wings are still the originals.

On the right wall of the nave facing us there is an expressive piece of carving showing the mourning of Christ (about 1500) and next to it the Altar of the Twelve Apostles (beginning of the 16th century, but the relief on the right was added later). The crucifix above is flanked by St. Mary and St. John. Opposite, there are four panel paintings, created by Michael Wolgemut around 1490, in addition to a statue of Sts. Anne and Mary with Jesus, produced by Veit Stoß or his workshop in about 1505.

The still existing shields document a rite practiced by the members of the Teutonic Order. Prior to admission to the order, each candidate had to provide proof that he was a descendant of a knight, with witnesses swearing an oath. Some of the old tombstones of knights of the order, e.g. that of Konrad von Egloffstein (d. 1416), are also reminiscent of the time the church served as place of worship of the order. The Minnesänger and poet Thannhäuser was knight of the Teutonic Order in Nuremberg from about 1250 to 1261. It is presumed that he was buried in St. James' Church.

Let us now take a closer look at the church of **St. Elisabeth**. After the Teutonic Order had the former Gothic church demolished in 1785, they built the neoclassical central building with its 50 meter high cupola. When the Order was dissolved in 1809, however, the interior of the church remained in an unfinished state. The final work was not completed until 1902–1905 when the church was given to the Catholic community as second parish church of the Old Town. The cross of the Teutonic Order appears on the cupola and reminds us of its builders. They were the only ones allowed to hold a Catholic mass in their place of worship after the Reformation in Nuremberg (1525). To the right, the hospital building adjoins the church. It served as soldiers' barracks in the 19th century and today houses the police headquarters. Apart from the church and the hospital building, only the grain store to the rear of the complex was left after the damage caused during the war.

St. James' Church: panel paintings created by Michael Wolgemut in 1490

The Spittlertor (Spittler Gate) and Rochusfriedhof (St. Roche´s Cemetery)

(Extended Tour)

Ludwigstraße leading from St. James' Church brings us to the **Spittlertor**, one of four round, mighty gate towers including the gun yard. In front of it there is a traffic junction, a ring road around the old part of the city, called Plärrer. The name originates from the Middle High German word "plarre" which means "free space" where entertainment for the people, including a circus took place. This is where the first German train started in 1835, the Ludwig train, going in the direction of Fürth. The locomotive "Adler" and the engine driver, William Wilson, were from England.

Rothenburgerstraße, half right to the direction just taken, leads to the **Rochusfriedhof** (St. Roche´s Cemetery) after about 300 m. In 1518, after the town council had forbidden burials to take place within the city walls, this cemetery was laid out for the dead of the Lorenz side of the town.

The uniform size and shape of the gravestones – which we observe at the Johannisfriedhof (St. John's Cemetery) for the Sebaldus District as well – had been determined precisely in 1522 as a symbol of equality in death. The only visible differences are seen in the quality of the cast bronze tablets from the 16th to 18th centuries which indicate name, profession and the insignia of the deceased. Grave no. 90 contains the remains of the famous bronze-founder, Peter Vischer, creator of the tomb of St. Sebald, and his sons.

The **Rochuskapelle** (St. Roche´s Chapel) was built in 1520 and was an endowment by the patrician, Konrad Imhoff. The artistic stained glass (1521) is by Veit Hirsvogel and has remained intact to this day. Inside, there are three remarkable altars, the Rosenkranzaltar, (Altar of the Rosary, 1522), the side altar to the north and the main altar (about 1521), whose panel paintings reveal the influence of Albrecht Dürer.

22

The DB Museum – Verkehrsmuseum Nürnberg (Nuremberg Transport Museum) and Museum für Kommunikation (Museum of Communication) (not included in the tour)

The Transport Museum is reached most easily from this point of our tour and is therefore described in this part of the guide, although a visit does require some time.

Walking through Kartäusergasse along the west side of the German National Museum and through the Kartäusertor (Carthusian Gate), we cross Ringstraße, turn into Lessingstraße and arrive at the museum's visitors' entrance. Two independent museums exist here under one and the same roof. The **DB Museum** (Museum of the German Railway) and the Museum für Kommunikation (Museum of Communication) in the **Verkehrsmuseum** (Transport Museum). The former is the oldest German railway museum and arose from a collection of model vehicles from the Royal Bavarian Railway, displayed at the National Trade Exhibition in Nuremberg between 1882 and 1892. The museum moved into the present building in 1925. The museum was completely re-arranged for its 1985 anniversary and to this end one room was dedicated to the history of the railway. Models, pictures, drawings, slide shows and scenes were set up to demonstrate the various epochs of railway development.

In two of the exhibition halls there are numerous originals on show which include locomotives of varying horsepower and their carriages as well as the Pullmann saloon which once belonged to the fairy-tale figure of King Ludwig II of Bavaria and also that used by Prince Bismarck. There is also a reconstruction of the first German locomotive, the "Adler," with its carriages. The originals have been replaced by models on a scale 1:10 in keeping with this internationally most comprehensive collection of model vehicles.

The **Museum für Kommunikation** is one of the oldest museums on technological history in Europe and displays its collections on the 2nd and 3rd floors of the museum building in Lessingstraße covering an area of about 2000 sqm. The objects shown present the development of the post and communication taking into account Bavarian postal history from five centuries. Carriages and vehicles, travel utensils and equipment, technical devices from early telegraphs to the modern telephone reflect the history of the post and transmission of news from the Middle Ages until the present. Different devices, from a Morse telegraph to a telephone exchange device, invite the visitor to test them. Varying exhibitions give a deeper insight into the manifold aspects of human communication.

KIBALA, all for children
Trains of the old and
new generation

DB Museum
Lessingstr. 6, Tel. 0 18 04/44 22 33,
e-mail: wener.holub@bku.db.de,
Internet: www.dbmuseum.de,
open Tuesday-Sunday 9 a.m. – 5 p.m.

Museum für Kommunikation
Lessingstr. 6, Tel. 09 11/2 30 88 85,
e-mail: mk.nuernberg@t-online.de,
Internet: www.museumsstiftung.de,
open Tuesday to Sunday 9 a.m. – 5 p.m.

On the Way to Neutor (New Gate)

Dr.-Kurt-Schuhmacher-Straße runs between Jakobsplatz and the White Tower. We follow this street in a north-western direction and leave the Old Town by its West Gate. Those who enjoy a moment of contemplation will take the footpath in front of the keep in the direction of the castle. An even better view perhaps is to be gained from the sidewalk next to the busy street. The liberal proportions of the sentry walk at this point of the main wall have been extended and are used as a residential area. We see here that the city fortifications which include the **Schlayerturm** (Schlayer Tower) and a bastion served to secure both bridges over the river Pegnitz. The wall of the keep was built around the round tower of the New Gate as an angular entrenchment in the course of extension works in 1563/64.

Town fortification at the western outflow of the River Pegnitz and so-called Schlayer Tower (1422)

At the Johannisfriedhof (St. John's Cemetery)

At this point we can pause to mark out another route. Johannisstraße goes on beyond the driveway under the gate and leads out for about the distance of a kilometer to St. John's Cemetery. In many ways it is similar to St. Roche's Cemetery, but it also served the neighboring infirmary and the villages around during the 13th century as a last resting place for their inhabitants. After 1518, however, it served as cemetery for the Sebaldus district. More than at St. Roche's Cemetery one finds famous names on

Magnificent flowers on the tombstones in front of St. John's Church

the bronze epitaphs of the gravestones lying flat on the ground. Albrecht Dürer, for example, is buried here (grave 649), as are Veit Stoß (268), Veit Hirsvogel (903), Willibald Pirckheimer (1414) and Anselm Feuerbach (715) to name perhaps the most famous.

In the middle of all these sarcophagus-type tombstones we find the **Johanniskirche** (St. John's Church) rising up among them which, apart from its sacristy (15th century), has been here since 1395. The side panels of the main altar are adorned by paintings by Dürer's pupil, Wolf Traut. Features also worth seeing are the tabernacle (about 1380) , the small side altar (about 1440) as well as several epitaphs. Another building of interest is the late Gothic round edifice of the **Holzschuher-Kapelle** (Holzschuher Chapel) which is situated on the east side of the cemetery. It contains the last great work of art created by Adam Kraft (1508) and depicts the burial of Christ. This in fact concludes the Way of the Cross which the artist is presumed to have begun on commission of the Bamberg knight, Heinrich Marschalk von Rauheneck, at the Pilatushaus.

We turn back in the direction of the Old Town. In the 16th, 17th and 18th centuries, numerous gardens, the so-called Gardens of the Hesperides were situated close to the cemetery. Their name originates from the orange and lemon collections displayed here, and hints at the antique legend of Heracles, whose actions included stealing golden apples from the Garden of the Hesperides. Three of these Baroque gardens were reconstructed and form a charming ensemble together with the summer house.

Back at the Neutor we continue our way along the city's fortifications. The nearer we come to the city's castle, the more tortuous and re-inforced become the bastions. They start south-west of the Tiergärtnertorturm, the only tower without a round encasing. The city fathers had these fortifications built in the 16th century according to plans suggested by the Italian military architect, Antonio Fazuni, and incorporated the castle and its defensive installations into their plans. As we pass through the Vestnertor we find ourselves back in the castle keep and here we end our tour.

In the Wake of National Socialism

The name of this city is closely associated with the doings of the Nazis and their "Third Reich." Nuremberg was the place where Nazi Party Rallies were held, and it was here that the notorious Nuremberg Laws were conceived and later promulgated. Here, too, was where Julius Streicher, Gauleiter for Franconia, published his rabble-rousing, anti-Semitic paper, "Der Stürmer," and also the place where the so-called "Nuremberg Trials" were held.

The odd thing was, however, that there were fewer Nazis in the Franconian metropolis than elsewhere. Hitler's preference for Nuremberg was based on its earlier history, on the fact that it was once the scene of imperial diets and the place where the imperial insignia were in safe-keeping, the secret capital of the Holy Roman Empire of German Nations.

As early as August 1923, National Socialists and similarly orientated political groups celebrated their "German Day" with a march past Ludendorf, Hitler and Streicher on the Hauptmarkt, and in the same month the last published the first issue of his inflammatory paper from Pfannengasse No. 19. The first Nazi Party Rally was held in Nuremberg in 1927, the next in 1929, and every year in September from 1933 to 1938. In 1935, the Reichstag passed the "Nürnberger Gesetze" (Nuremberg Laws) at a special session which reduced German Jews to second-class citizens.

A short time after seizing power in 1933, Hitler decreed that Nuremberg was to be the setting for National Socialist Party Rallies "for time immemorial." A gigantic building project was then initiated in the area of the Dutzendteich (Dozen Ponds) to the south-east of the city. More than 130 firms worked for the "Zweckverband Reichsparteitag Nürnberg" (Association for the National Socialist Party Rally Grounds Nuremberg). One of the most extensive projects was the Märzfeld (March Field), a parade ground comprising 60 hectares, surrounded by 28 towers, each 40 meters high. The "Deutsche Stadion" (German Stadium) was planned to seat 405,000 spectators but never got past foundation work. The **Great Avenue**, 60 m wide and about 2 km long, as the north-western prolongation of the central axis of the National Socialist Party Rally Grounds, is aligned directly with Nuremberg Castle as symbol of the old Empire. Today, the Great Avenue is used as parking lot for the hundreds of buses which come to Nuremberg for the Christmas Market.

The new **Congress Hall**, a horseshoe-shaped building (275 m long, 265 m wide) of gigantic proportions was only half finished, in particular the spectator tribunes and a pillar-free roof. Designed in accordance with the "Colosseum" in Rome, it was to provide space for 50,000 people. Nowadays it is partly used as storage hall. The southern building serves as domicile for the Nuremberg Symphony Orchestra.

In the northern building, the **Dokumentationszentrum Reichsparteitagsgelände** (Documentation Center of the

The "Documentation Center of the National Socialist Party Rally Grounds" inaugurated in 2001 in the northern building of the Congress Hall

National Socialist Party Rally Grounds) has existed since November 2001. The outer structure was built accord-

Dokumentationszentrum Reichsparteitagsgelände

Bayernstr. 110, Tel. 09 11/2 31-56 66, e-mail: dokumentationszentrum@ref4. stadt.nuernberg.de, Internet: www.museen. nuernberg.de, open Monday to Friday 9 a.m. – 6 p.m., Sunday 10 a.m. – 6 p.m.

ing to plans by the architect, Günther Domenig, from Graz. With his architectural arrangement consisting of steel and glass he created a convincing contrast to the Nazi architecture. A 130 m long glass hallway passes through the building diagonally. On the upper floor, the permanent exhibition "Fascination and Power" is displayed. Next to this, the study forum offers seminar rooms for school classes, youth and adult groups who wish to delve more intensively into the history of National Socialism.

The monumental Congress Hall was never completed

Grandstand of the Zeppelinfeld

On the other side of the Dutzendteich, the remains of the grandstand of the **Zeppelinfeld** (1935–37) are slowly disintegrating almost unused. The famous Norisring race attracts crowds to the tribunes once a year. This is where once 130 anti-aircraft searchlights radiated a pillar of light about 8 km high into the dark sky. Hitler held his speech for the masses from the small projecting section of the tribune – as in 1938 when far more than half a million followers came to Nuremberg.

For them the "Führer" brought back the imperial insignia from their repository in Vienna to Nuremberg and had them put on display in the former St. Catherine's Church. Hitler resided in the hotel "Deutscher Hof," Frauentorgraben 29, on the southern border of the old city next to the opera house.

The destiny of National Socialist rule was fulfilled in the **Palace of Justice** in Fürther Straße 110, to the west of the Old Town, Court Room 600. On the occasion of the famous Nuremberg Trials the main defendants were detained in the adjoining prison behind the court building. Hermann Göring, cell 413, avoided execution of the death sentence by committing suicide.

The others who had been condemned to death, among them Julius Streicher, publisher of the anti-Semitic newspaper "Der Stürmer," ended on the gallows in the early morning hours of October 16, 1946 which had been erected in the sports hall (since torn down) of the Nuremberg prison. The bodies of the executed were then cremated in a Munich crematorium, and their ashes were dispersed in a side arm of the River Isar.

Schwurgerichtssaal 600

Landgericht Nürnberg-Fürth,
Fürther Str. 110,
Tel. 09 11/2 31-54 21,
e-mail: museen@stadt.nuernberg.de,
Internet: www.museen.nuernberg.de,

guided tours:
Saturday, Sunday 1, 2, 3, 4 p.m.

The Christmas Market

The **Christmas Market** in Nuremberg goes back to the beginning of the 17th century, and was celebrated then as now shortly before Christmas. It is Germany's oldest Christmas Market. Its origins can be traced back to a custom

The Frauenkirche and the Beautiful Fountain are a pleasant background for the famous Christmas Market

introduced by Martin Luther, that of giving children presents at Christmas. In a similar way, the stands – a total of

about 150 – still offer toys and Christmas decorations in every conceivable variation but also local specialties such as "Zwetschgemännla" (dolls made of prunes), "Hutzel-brot" (spiced currant bread) and "Lebkuchen" (ginger-bread). Among the sales stands, numerous snack boo-ths tempt the visitor with mulled wine and sausages.

The Church of Our Lady and the Beautiful Fountain form the incomparable backdrop for this market which is ope-ned on the Friday before the first Sunday in Advent. The famous Nuremberg Holy Child speaks the prolog from the balcony of the Church of Our Lady and invites all children to come to the Christmas Market and look forward joyfully to the great event of the birth of Christ.

This market attracts about 2 million visitors each year who come to Nuremberg from near and far. Whoever wishes to avoid what is often too great a crowding and can arrange his or her time accordingly, should visit the Nuremberg Christmas Market in the morning, or towards evening time for a leisurely stroll. On the nearby Hans Sachs Square, a Christmas Market for children was established a few years ago, with the opportunity of playing, riding the carousel, listening to fairy tales and getting into the spirit of the Christmas feast.

Christkindlesmarkt:

Friday before the 1st Sunday of Advent until Dec. 24th 2 p.m.
Monday to Wednesday 9 a.m. – 8 p.m.,
Thursday to Saturday 9 a.m. – 9 p.m.,
Sunday 10.30 a.m. – 8 p.m.

Around Nuremberg

The neighboring city of **Fürth** only reveals its architectural qualities to the careful observer. Up to the beginning of the last century, the peasants' marketplaces served as a bone of contention between three territorial lords, namely, the bishops of Bamberg, the Margraves of Ansbach and the imperial city of Nuremberg. When Fürth fell to Bavaria in 1806 and later, in 1835, when the first German railway line ran through here to Nuremberg, the town rapidly developed into an important industrial and commercial city. Picturesque farms with Franconian half-timbering as, for example, the idyllic Stadlerhof, delightful little corners and lanes as well as prestigious house fronts such as those seen on the Hornschuchpromenade (about 1827), the Stadttheater (1901–02) and Burgfarnbacher Castle (1830–34), today the city's museum, are harmoniously integrated into the modern city scene.

The city's many sports facilities have contributed to the fact that the town has gone down in the annals of sport history. The SpVgg Fürth won the German football championship three times, and gymnasts and athletes have also won gold medals at the Olympic Games.

There are walking paths through the surrounding parks and countryside which also includes the delightful Stadtwald following the broad course of the river valley. The numerous local festivals culminate in the Kirchweih, which is presumed to have been celebrated since the consecration of St. Michael's Church (11th/12th centuries). Today's ceremony with the Thanksgiving procession developed after the 30 Years' War and attracts more than 100,000 spectators each year.

About 15 km further north, settled between what is known as Franconia's Switzerland, Steigerwald and Knoblauchsland, lies the university and industrial city of **Erlangen**, a center of research and technology and the place of birth of the physicist, Georg Simon Ohm. Cozy student pubs, restaurants offering local food and specialty restaurants vie to please local and non-local guests. The town offers

3000 beds to its visitors. The city's Congress Hall (Kongresszentrum) at the very center of the town is easily accessible by 7 direct highway connections from every direction and also from Nuremberg's airport. The center of the town possesses a large castle garden surrounded by attractive Baroque houses and the Markgrafen Theater, the oldest theater presenting Baroque plays in southern Germany. There is a 180 km long network of cycling paths which passes through fir woods, cherry orchards and tobacco and potato fields in the surrounding area. Those wishing to see northern Bavaria's most beautiful festival should visit Erlangen's Bergkirchweih. It has been celebrated for more almost 250 years on the beer cellars on Castle Hill.

Roughly 20 km to the south of Nuremberg lies the old gold beaters' town of **Schwabach** in which this unusual profession is still practiced. Commerce and industry are the basis for taking care of the treasures history has left to the town. We are impressed by the romantic Königsplatz (King's Square) with the "Beautiful Well" (1716), we look at the City Hall and high-gabled citizens' houses where princes languished both as prisoners and guests, for instance Goethe, who stayed here overnight three times.

Also worth seeing is the Church of St. John and St. Martin (15th century) which was built with the help of Adam Kraft. The medieval shrine altar was created in Michael Wolgemut's workshop, with carved figures presumably from the circle of Veit Stoß. The stained glass for the choir windows was delivered by Veit Hirsvogel and his workshop.

Remainders of the city's ancient fortifications such as the Hördlertor (Hördler Gate) with its old linden-tree round off the complete character of this little town. Nice walking tours take you to the Schwabach and Rednitz Valley, to Heidenberg, through meadows and woods, through a countryside which is as friendly and hospitable as the little town itself.

Together with Nuremberg, Fürth and Erlangen, Schwabach forms an important axis along the European Canal running through beautiful Franconia.